ACKNOWLEDGMENTS

The book, <u>Sales Hack</u>, is a "Hackathon" powered by more than 25 of the world's greatest *Sales Hacks* alive today! While preparing to launch the book, we discovered that the easiest way to lead is to jump in front of a parade. We are committed to facilitate the contribution of sales hacks on an ongoing basis to advance the profession of selling through www.SalesHack.com.

As Gerhard Gschwandtner, CEO of Selling Power, kindly said, "Chad and Chris are leading the movement of Sales Velocity and the authors share the same mindset which represents the Zeitgeist of our time: we are all co-creators of our future and we are surfing the crest of a wave that will revolutionize the world as we know it. The new formula for winning is to integrate velocity in salespeople's mindsets, skill sets and tool sets."

DEDICATION

This Book is Dedicated to the Most Timeless Practice of any
Sales Hack: The Cold Call (*By Kraig Kleeman*)

Has Cold Calling Collapsed?

Collapse: To fall or cave in; crumble suddenly.
-Source: Dictionary.com

Has cold calling collapsed? Has it caved in? Has it crumbled?

This trendy, but less than tidy discussion is being waged by naïve content mongers throughout all four corners of our sometimes great, *sometimes less than great*, cyber world.

Decreed by pseudo-intellectuals who possess mastery at unskilled argumentation, mostly made up of technology vendors and sales trainers who pick up their crumbs, this discussion is fraught with fallacy. These so-called thought leaders gain financially by attempting to convince all business folks in all industry sectors that their survival is dependent upon adoption of their inventions. *Translation:* A lot of horsepower is thrown at this false premise.

Pesky arithmetic is accepted and factual reality is largely ignored. It's a bit like Al Gore shouting to the media that "extreme weather events" are 100 times more common today than they were 30 years ago due to global warming. Gore's claims actually run counter to mounting scientific evidence that global warming is not making the weather more "extreme."

I often wonder, at times, if the advocates of the "death of cold calling" movement have mixed us a martini using battery acid instead of vermouth and somehow managed to make it pleasing to the palate. The argument appears delicious and intoxicating, but somehow its outcome creates a harmfully poisonous effect. Unwittingly, a tsunami of falsity has become accepted   as   factual   reality.

There is a mouse in the house.

Just as the degree of civilization of any society can be judged by entering its prisons, the degree of productive commerce can be judged, at least in part, by observing the detailed nuances of behavior associated with the adoption of speculation, versus the adoption of fact.

There is little doubt that the deployment of digital outreach provides a powerful platform for warming up cold prospects, and especially in finding "ready to buy" leads that are highly valuable. Email marketing, social medium channels, cyber blogging, V-logging, and SEO activities are, in many ways, a 21st century technological phenomena of "direct-response" activity. These venues are the backbone for a new generation of multiples of new-world Montgomery Wards and new-world Sears & Roebucks. The result is a lot of goodness in the realm of commerce.

Let us not forget, however, that small business is the real backbone of America's economy. That said, try telling a broker of refurbished airplane parts that raw list cold calling is not a vital activity for revenue capture. Try telling most any seller in the financial services industry that raw list cold calling to potential investors is not working. Try telling a manufacturer of plumbing, HVAC, and home improvement products that cold calling aimed at resellers and end users is ineffective. You just might need a degree in martial arts or unfettered access to the US military's drone missile fleet to defend yourself.

When coupled with good technique, a raw list of good data and a generic telephone is still quite the effective tool for gaining access to target buyers.

But on another note (quite literally) folk-rock songwriter Bob Dylan may be the most prolific artistic writer in modern history. Over the course of five decades his lyrics have incorporated a variety of political, social, philosophical, and literary influences. His work has defied existing pop music conventions. It has demonstrated enormous appeal to truth seeking individuals wishing to avoid fads, trends, and general falsities.

In closing, it is my honor to prepare you for an amalgamation of egalitarianism: A collection of well written sales hack pieces. Though the content you are about to read may represent differing views and at times even seem disparate one from another, the content is written by some of the most thought-provoking thought leaders in modern business history.

Alas I leave you to enjoy this super content with lyrics from the song that Bob Dylan has performed on stage more than any other throughout his illustrious, lengthy, seemingly prophetic career.

Let us not talk falsely now, for the hour is getting late.
-Discography: *All Along the Watchtower*Bob Dylan, Columbia Records, 1967

FOREWORD

Imagine if you grew up thinking that you would one day become a great sales professional. You sell things as a child, you continue to sell things in high school, and when you get to college you become the President of the American Marketing Association at your university. To top it off, you create an advertising sales role for yourself and sell thousands of dollars in advertising for the university campus television station.

Then you graduate from college, take your first real sales position, and relocate to Phoenix, Arizona. You order your business cards, throw on a suit and tie, and your career in sales is about to blossom, right? **Wrong.**

Within 9 months you are **FIRED!** You feel like your boss just took you out back and left your cold, blue, lifeless body for dead. To make matters worse, you now have many doubts about your ability as a sales professional, and are shipped back to your parents house to think it all over and determine if sales is the right career for you.

This is MY story.

And after twenty years of professional selling, I have become a lifelong learner. My hope for you is that whether you are a seasoned executive or an entry level Sales Development Representative, that you will gain value from <u>Sales Hack</u>.

CONTENTS

THE 8 BONUS SALES HACKS

SALES HACKS CONTRIBUTED BY

Lauren Bailey
Ralph Barsi
Chris Beall
Trish Bertuzzi
Matt Behrend
Rick Bennett
Chad Burmeister
Stephen D'Angelo
David DiStefano
Jourdan DuFort
Jim Eberlin
Shawn Elledge
Gerhard Gschwandtner
Richard Harris
Alice Heiman
Liz Heiman
Matt Heinz
Kraig Kleeman
Mark Kosoglow
Dave Kurlan
Dan McDade
Skip Miller
Mike O'Neil
Andy Paul
Bob Perkins
Larry Reeves
Steve Richard
Lori Richardson
Craig Rosenberg
Tibor Shanto
Kurt Shaver
Gabe Villamizar
Townsend Wardlaw

WHAT IS A SALES HACK?

In advance of launching this book, a group of more than 25 of the world's best "sales hackers" collaborated on pulling together various "sales hacks" to share with other sales professionals. When looking for the definition of "Sales Hack", we discovered that the existing definitions didn't fully articulate what a Sales Hack really is.

What is a Sales Hack?

Hacker - A "hacker" is someone who thinks outside of the box, disregards the rules, and discovers new ways to solve problems.

Sales Hacker – Thinks outside of the box, disregards the rules, and solves the biggest problem of all – outselling their competitors.

Sales Hack – The solutions discovered when a Sales Hacker thinks outside of the box, disregards the rules, and finds something new that changes the way sellers can outsell the competition.

SALES HACK #1
SELLING TO BONO

It had been a long, arduous two weeks of airports, limos, meetings, training sessions, and public speaking throughout central Europe. I was utterly exhausted. In spite of my body running on empty, I was excited that it was Friday afternoon. I was scheduled to fly to Greece's Mykonos Island for some fun in the sun, good food, and general relaxation with my brother. After all, how often are we both in Europe at the same time for business reasons? Not so much!

I was on my way to the airport in Brussels with Heaven on my mind and then came the dreaded phone call. My brother dropped the bomb on me. As Chief Revenue Officer for a publicly traded software company, he had a multi-million dollar deal on the line with a large bank based in Amsterdam. His CEO ordered him to stay in Amsterdam as long as necessary to get the deal. Translation: "Don't come home until the deal is signed. Camp out on the dude's doorstep. Don't take no for an answer. We need this $6.5 million dollar deal to boost our stock." Typical CEO talk. You get the picture.

I thought about forging ahead to Mykonos on my own. After all, Keith Richards is rumored to hang out there often. As a hard core Rolling Stones fan, the idea of even remotely spotting Keith Richards, rock's ultimate Bad Boy, was intriguing to say the least. Notwithstanding, I didn't have it in me to abandon my brother, and little did I know that a much more prominent rock icon would emerge in my presence in Amsterdam.

Alas, I boarded a high-speed train from Brussels to Amsterdam and arrived safely. I always enjoy warm, summer nights in Amsterdam, but this particular night I was simply worn-out. I wanted three things prior to lights out and bedtime: (i) my hotel room, (ii) privacy, and (iii) a cold beverage. I arrived at the 5-star hotel in Leidseplein Square that my brother's executive assistant had organized for us. Within 3 minutes of hotel check-in my head hit the pillow and I was out like a lamp. About an hour later, the phone rang. It was my brother suggesting that we go out and yuck it up in Amsterdam. Let's face it, Leidseplein Square is one of Amsterdam's popular centers for nightlife with theaters, cafes, restaurants, cinemas, the casino, and more. Street musicians, jugglers, fire-eaters and other performers make the square a lively place until the early hours, especially on a warm summer evening. I was not tempted to enter into the nightlife, however. I was simply exhausted from the events of the week. I finally decided that visiting the lounge would be the quickest route to food and drink, and I would fulfill my brotherly duties to hook up for a short time and then head back to my room for some needed rest. After all, we had the balance of the weekend for seeing the sights and yucking it up. I spruced myself up, splashed on some cologne and made my way down to the lounge. Little did I know that I was in for the experience of a lifetime.

Here's what happened: While catching up with my brother and sipping on my beverage, I heard some commotion near the entrance of the lounge where we were relaxing. I looked over to see what was happening. Were my eyes deceiving me? I had to do a double take. It was true. In

walked Bono. Yes, Bono, as in U2's front man. Yes, Bono, as in the greatest rock performer in history. In a word, I was overwhelmed.

After pinching myself and realizing this was not a dream, my brother and I experienced some serious laughter watching what happened over the next 30 minutes or so. Every time someone new walked into the lounge and realized that Bono was "in the house", they would approach him for an autograph or something similar. Each time that happened, Bono's embedded bodyguard would emerge out of nowhere and explain to his autograph seekers that Bono is not feeling well and is not available for fan club time at this moment. We really chuckled as we watched the varying approaches utilized by these groupies:

- The intelligent groupie would simply say something like, "Hey Bono, I've been a big fan for 10 years. How about an autograph?" Enter body guard who politely but firmly stops the groupie in his tracks.

- The stoner groupie who probably just visited the infamous Bulldog Café from across the street would say something like, "Hey Bono. D-u-u-u-de! When you wrote that song 'Where the Streets Have No Name' was it, like a re-e-e-e-ligious experience d-u-u-ude..?" Enter body guard who maintains politeness but makes it clear that the stoner is about to be smacked down if he doesn't leave the premises NOW!

Let's face it, Bono is one of the most in-demand persons on the planet. If he wants some down time, he deserves it.

After a few cold beverages Karry started a debate about who would have the greater legacy, the Beatles or U2. We debated the point for a while and then switched to arguing over which U2 album was the best.

Painful as it was, people continued to approach Bono's table over and over again without ever catching Bono's attention, only to be escorted away by a member of his entourage. I was laughing at the utter hopelessness of the attempts when Karry made a wager.

"Kraig, you claim in your sales transformation practice to be able to win meetings with all sorts of global heads of business and C-Level executives, right?" he asked.

"Yes. When leading with fact-based research and appealing to your target buyers' professional mandates, it works with an amazing conversion rate yield every time."

"Right," I replied politely but with some reserved skepticism.

"Well," he continued, "I bet you can't get a fifteen minute meeting with Bono right now."

"Karry, don't be ridiculous. Where have you been for the last thirty minutes? Bono is not interested in meeting with anyone right now."

"I thought you said your system works every time. Are you saying it can't work now? I mean you're approximately 20 feet from BONO dude. Win a meeting now!" He was trying to get at me and it was working.

"Alright," I said defensively, "What should we bet?"

"If you can get a meeting with Bono, right now, that lasts more than 3 minutes I will pay for your hotel and all your expenses for the weekend. If you can't you pay for mine."

This was the sort of reckless brotherly competition that had characterized our relationship since we were young boys. I knew from past experience that I had no choice on the matter. I either had to accept the challenge or concede failure. The expenses would no doubt be in the multiples of thousands of dollars for the weekend, as we were staying at a rockstar, 5-star hotel and we were planning to hit the coolest restaurants and clubs in Amsterdam, not to mention the scheduled private car to take us to all of the historical museums on Saturday. There was no way I was going to back down from this challenge.

I needed a strategy. I knew that unless I had something different than these other groupies I was going to end up receiving the same patronizing look I had been giving to everyone else who failed. And then it hit me. I already have a proven strategy. One of the core principles of my selling methodology, The Must-React System, is to take yourself out of the sales process. You have to remove yourself from the normal noise that your target is always hearing.

The best way to do that is by tapping into the core values / professional mandates of your target buyer with whom you want to win a meeting. After winning the meeting, well-equipped sellers are empowered to navigate a highly charged, fact-based research presentation that is centered in topics, trends, metrics, and outcomes. In fact, I learned early in my practice that this is the most pivotal principle in mastering the enterprise sale. I began to ponder the obvious question: What is of core importance to Bono? What are his personal and professional mandates? Being a long-time fan of U2, and having admired Bono's personal life, I queried myself regarding Bono's passions, life goals, etc. I decided that it would not be a good idea to approach him on the basis of his music, since he gets approached dozens of times daily on that topic. My mind harkened back to articles I have read in the past about his deliberate involvement in a variety of humanitarian efforts which includes fighting AIDS and other social issues that plague underdeveloped nations and underprivileged people groups. I recalled that Bono had visited the White House, donated extraordinary amounts of money, and articulated his views on a number of TV news shows. He has had audiences with heads of state, wealthy entrepreneurs, and the most famous of the famous people on Earth. I recall reading some of his public speeches where he described himself as a voice for "defending the poor of the earth."

After some thought, I decided that my only chance at getting a meeting with Bono was no different than getting a meeting with a senior executive at any global 2000 company: I had to appeal to a topic that is absolutely core to his thinking! Bono is an amazing musician. He knows it and everyone tells him that. But what he cares about, what keeps him up at night, is his compassion for the poor and hurting throughout the world.

I geared myself up for one shot to grab his attention on an issue that mattered.

"Hey Bono!" I shouted over to the bar.

His face looked my way.

"I want you to know how much I admire the way you defend the poor of the earth."

His ears now perked up! In fact, his countenance beamed angelically.

I continued, "I once was on the board of directors for an outreach to abandoned children in South America and I understand how painfully difficult it is to get individuals from our modernized world to understand the plight of lesser developed nations and lesser privileged people groups!"

I lifted my drink and continued.

"And I just want to toast you for your steadfast commitment to defending the poor of the earth!"

From approximately twenty feet away Bono lifted his cup in a toast with me.

At first, that was it. Nothing happened right away so I sat down and began to think about how Karry was going to spend the rest of the weekend spending my money and rubbing my failure in my face. But then I noticed that Bono was talking to a member of his entourage. The man came over and told me that Bono would like to invite me to his table for a cold beverage!

I ended up talking with him for approximately an hour. We discussed how his passion for charitable work originated, recent news, and a new campaign for AIDS prevention in Africa and China. We were able to discuss a variety of topics that would have never been possible had I not been invited to his table. This is called *Leading with Fact-Based Research* and *Appealing to Your Target Buyers' Professional Mandates* in sales methodology phraseology. But never once did either of us speak a word about music. It was all about his interests in bringing genuine assistance to the "poor of the earth."

Why did Bono meet with me, even though many others had tried to meet with him in that moment? Why did he accept my request? Mostly because I did not approach him on the same basis that everyone else approaches him, which is "as a fan of his music". Rather, I approached him on the basis of what is ABSOLUTELY CORE to his personal and professional mandates. People are much more inclined to discuss topics near and dear to their hearts than they are to discuss sterile, innocuously boring topics. And while Bono has an astonishing track record of creating amazing music mixed with powerful lyrics, this is not the topic where his heart is most tightly bound. His heart is bound up in organizing humanitarian relief for people, groups, nations, and the poor of the earth.

The number one problem with most sales people is that they are too self-centered. This isn't a moral critique; it's a professional one. Sales people grab onto a great story or benefit of their product and they insist on telling it to their customers and prospects. Even if the prospect is obviously not interested, many sales people will continue to blunder their way through the same canned phrases and glory stories until the client leaves or hangs up. They don't take the time to understand how and why their client would be interested in this information.

As true as that is, the top decision makers in sales and marketing organizations are even worse. They are completely infatuated with their products' abilities and the customer list that they have. They have the feeling that just because they have been able to convince other large companies to purchase their solution everyone else should just flock to them instinctively. They produce flashy, glossy, product centric e-mail blasts and marketing collateral. So much of this effort is devoted to a "keeping up with the Jones's" mentality. If my competitor's product can go fast, mine can go faster. This type of prospecting is the equivalent of the rejected groupies in the bar with Bono. Buyers are *initially* less interested in what your product does. They are interested in outcomes, not features.

The power of persuasion depends entirely on your sales organization's ability to understand your prospective clients' core values / professional mandates. If you cannot define this and appeal to them based upon an authentic understanding, your conversion rates and revenue capture rates will suffer. And suffer much. Bono is a rock star but his core value is 'defending the poor of the earth'. Since thousands of fans across the world have praised him for his music, it would be foolish for me to lump myself in with the thousands of other 'fans'. Instead, by appealing to one of the deepest issues of Bono's concern, I became perceived as a fellow soldier in his battle against world poverty. I wasn't one of thousands. I was someone who understood what *really* matters.

The entire experience was the real thing. Even better than the real thing!

Sales Hack contributed by Kraig Kleeman, The World's Greatest Cold Caller, KraigKleeman.com & Forbes Top Sales Expert

Kraig Kleeman is the World's Greatest Cold Caller. In the past 10 years he has architected the entire selling model for more than 50 cloud based computing companies, and more than 75 companies from other industries. From 2011 – 2014, sellers that were trained and certified in The Must-React System by Kraig Kleeman completed 1 million outreaches, scheduled 252,000 meetings (mostly with senior executives) and generated more than $400 million in net new revenue.

Kraig was founder and CEO of Express Direct, a technology company that sold digital pre-press solutions for high-end graphics designers. Kraig and his management team grew the company from $0 – $25 million annual revenue in less than four years. During that rapid growth period, Kraig had responsibility for 25 professional sellers who completed more than 1 million sales presentations under his care. It was during this critical time of need to validate the plan and exceed corporate growth expectations that Kraig developed *The Must-React System*, the world's most predictable and efficient selling methodology.

After selling the company, Kraig took a few years off from the traditional work world doing humanitarian outreach work in South America and Southeast Asia. At that time he authored the book *The Must-React System*. In the past seven years Kraig has maintained a global sales transformation consulting practice. During his tenure as a Global Sales Strategist, Kraig has documented the findings of 25,000 distinct sales presentations across 46 different professional sales organizations.

The results of Kraig's research is remarkable.

Kraig is recognized as the world's leading expert on sales process, sales transformation, and professional motivation. He is founder of KragKleemanTV, the world's most instructional sales training YouTube Channel. Kraig is one of the most sought after speakers in the world.

Kraig has had the pleasure of speaking on panels / forums with President George W. Bush, British Prime Minister Tony Blair, Silicon Valley Guru Guy Kawasaki, and others.

SALES HACK #2
THE INSIDE SALES HACK

In the late 80s and 90s and through the early 2000s, inside sales was deployed predominately in a team model supporting the field sales force. Today senior sales leaders know what inside sales knew many years ago. The digital and virtual way of doing business has arrived and is here to stay. In fact, traditional field salespeople have adopted some of the very same strategies and tactics that inside salespeople have been using for years. Why? Because buyers are demanding it. It should be no surprise then to see inside sales growing at a rate 3 times faster than field sales.

Extensive AA-ISP (American Association of Inside Sales Professionals) research in 2013 and 2014 indicated a significant shift from inside sales simply supporting field reps to carrying a discrete quota and responsibility over a set of accounts. From 2010 to 2014, companies moving inside sales from a teamed support role into a "discrete" quota-carrying model rose from 32% to over 50%. The AA-ISP forecasts that the discrete model will overtake the time-tested "team selling" model in the next few years.

Further, research by ZS Associates and Reality Works in the fall of 2014 indicated that 40% of large companies (greater than $1B in annual revenue) in the technology space are specifically shifting headcount from the field to inside sales.

Simply stated, virtual selling is alive and thriving. Face-to-face is on the decline.

Sales Hack contributed by: Bob Perkins, Founder & Chairman, The American Association of Inside Sales Professionals

A nationally-recognized inside sales innovator, Bob Perkins has extensive executive experience building and leading highly successful inside sales organizations. During his career he has created unique inside sales systems and structures, including team selling models, compensation plans, rewards and recognition programs, performance management tools, and sales campaigns which have been adopted by many of the nation's largest companies.

SALES HACK #3
SALES DNA: IS SALES FOR ME?

George was at the house today and he asked what kind of work I did. When he learned that I was a sales expert he told me that he tried selling cars once, wasn't very good at it, and so he quit. "I went to the same training as everyone else, sold the same products as everyone else, had the same management as everyone else, but got different results. I don't know why I sucked, but I knew enough to get out."

I said, "I can tell you why you struggled. You're a nice guy and you want people to like you, right?"

"Yup."

"So you couldn't say, do or ask the things they taught you to do because it didn't feel right, right?

"Exactly!"

"You probably shop around and think things over when you buy things for yourself, right?"

"Yup."

"So none of the techniques to stop them from shopping or to stop them from thinking it over came from conviction, right?"

"Exactly!"

"You're a pretty trusting guy, right?"

"Yup."

"So when they told you they'd be back on Monday to buy the car, you believed them, right?"

"Exactly!"

"And you never handled rejection really well, did you?"

"Nope."

"So that's why you weren't any good as a car salesman, George."

"Thank you SO MUCH. I feel so much better knowing why."

"You're welcome."

Don't make the mistake of believing that this conversation only relates to selling cars. These are a handful of the common reasons why salespeople struggle, and what's worse is that many of the salespeople who are IN sales today and struggling have these among dozens of other issues getting in their way.

If you are in sales and struggling, or considering sales and can relate to this conversation, then its possible that sales may not be the best fit for you. There are some professions from which moving to sales almost always has a bad ending - as if you were attempting to dive into a 4 foot deep swimming pool – with the new salesperson banging his head against a wall:

- Purchasing
- Teaching
- Social Work
- Scientist

Traits that make a successful sales professional

Many people have theories about the traits of successful salespeople. I sometimes refer to the elite 6% of salespeople, the next 20% and the bottom 74%. I took a new look at the data on the more than 900,000 salespeople have been assessed by Objective Management Group. Behavioral scientists would look at the data on the top 6% and report on some common findings. It might look like this:

<u>Top Salespeople have the following common characteristics</u>:

1. They enjoy selling
2. They prospect consistently
3. They have a strong Outlook

Of course, there are many more, but the problem I always have with these studies is that they don't look at the characteristics of the salespeople who are failing. Would you be surprised to know that the bottom 5% of all salespeople also have these characteristics? Well, they do. A more interesting comparison would be to look at the characteristics where we might find the biggest differences between the top 6% and the bottom 5%:

Top 5%	Trait	Bottom 5%
99.5%	Trainable and Coachable	0%
100%	Strong Desire for Sales Success	0%
95%	Strong Commitment to Sales Success	33%
94%	Don't Make Excuses for Results	20%
78%	Don't Need to be Liked by their Prospects	6%
59%	Don't Get Emotional	10%
98%	Comfortable Talking about Finances	2%
79%	Supportive Sales Beliefs	0%
76%	Supportive Buying Habits	8%
96%	Sales DNA of 80 or Better	0%
95%	Rejection Proof	18%
100%	Have Personal Written Goals	16%
95%	High Money Tolerance (choking point)	35%
88%	Make Decisions to Buy without Thinking it Over	18%
77%	% of the Attributes of a Hunter	31%
45%	% of the Attributes of a Closer	8%
59%	% of the Attributes of a Qualifier	11%

Wow, right?

You don't have to look much further than the impact of getting Desire wrong

There is a huge difference between the top and bottom performers but any individual finding is meaningless unless it is considered as part of the whole, in the context of what the salesperson will be selling, who they'll be selling it to, the anticipated resistance and the expected competition.

Despite the huge gap between the top and bottom groups, even the top group of salespeople falter in these areas:

- Only 50% are Motivated to earn more money - but that's because most of them have made so much already!

- Only 29% of them have a sales process they follow.
- As you saw from the data above, even this group has on average only 45% of the attributes of the closer competency. That just places more importance on the earlier stages of the sales process and reinforces what I so often say. If you slow down in the earliest stages of the sales process, the sales process will accelerate and closing will take care of itself.
- Only 34% of them are effective reaching top decision makers. They aren't a whole lot better in this area than their weak counterparts who reach top decision makers only 20% of the time.
- Only 43% of them are consistently uncovering the real budget so you know they are wasting some time as a result of that.
- Here's a shocker - despite the fact that 90% of them prospect consistently (although we don't define what "consistently" is), only 55% of them want to do it, so they force themselves. By contrast, 65% of the bottom 5% have the desire to prospect consistently, but only 82% actually prospect consistently.

With all of that said, successful salespeople must be able to develop capabilities in the following competencies:

- Hunting for new business (identifying, finding and adding opportunities to the pipeline)
- Consultative Approach to Selling (listening and asking questions, identifying compelling reasons to buy or move business to you, building a case)
- Qualifying Opportunities (making sure the opportunity is viable)
- Presentation (presenting the appropriate things, for the appropriate reasons, to the appropriate people, at the appropriate time)
- Closing (getting the deal signed)
- Posturing (favorable first impressions, ability to differentiate, be memorable)
- Intangibles (traits that cannot be taught, like award-winning personality, book of business, industry expert, etc.)

Selling skills can be learned and if you learn them correctly, practice consistently, apply and master them you can be successful as long as your Sales DNA supports the execution of those skills.

George and the rest of the bottom 5% have a flawed Sales DNA, which can't be taught. You can become aware of the weaknesses in your Sales DNA but if you have too many challenges with your Sales DNA, they tend to become insurmountable obstacles. On the other hand, even the top 6% have minor flaws in their Sales DNA and learn to work around those flaws. You can also simply decide to change your Sales DNA. It won't always be easy, but if succeeding in sales is important enough (Desire), you are willing to do what it takes to succeed (Commitment), you maintain a positive attitude and don't get down (Outlook) and take responsibility for your results or lack of them (Responsibility) you can and will make the changes necessary to succeed. Together, these elements are referred to as the Will to Sell. A Strong Will to Sell can have a positive impact on Sales DNA and as discussed, Sales DNA determines whether or not your selling skills can be executed consistently.

Sales Hack contributed by: Dave Kurlan, CEO, Objective Management Group and CEO, Kurlan & Associates

Dave Kurlan is a top-rated speaker, best selling author, radio show host, successful entrepreneur and sales development industry pioneer.

Dave is the founder and CEO of two companies which, between them, have been named four times to the Inc. 5000 list of fastest growing private companies. Objective Management Group (OMG) has been named the Top Sales Assessment Tool for 3 consecutive years. Kurlan & Associates is a global sales consulting firm.

He has written two books, including the best seller *Baseline Selling*, and contributed to many others, including *Stepping Stones*, with co-authors Deepak Chopra and Jack Canfield.

His Blog, *Understanding the Sales Force*, was named a Top Sales & Marketing Blog for 3 consecutive years, he was named a Top Sales & Marketing Influencer for 2012 and 2013, and was a 2012 inductee into the Sales & Marketing Hall of Fame.

SALES HACK #4
DEFINING A QUALIFIED LEAD

Having a common definition of a qualified lead is essential to effective lead to opportunity conversions in the funnel. But sadly too many organizations lack a clear definition of a qualified lead that is understood and followed by marketing and sales. When this happens, you see a breakpoint in the funnel. The lead flow passed from sales development reps (SDRs) to quota carrying sales reps is either too fast or too slow. Much like a car, your revenue engine either gets flooded with gas or chokes from lack of fuel. Either way the engine runs sub-optimally.

Sales and marketing leaders frequently ask Vorsight, "How should we define a qualified lead?" The classic consulting answer of "it depends" is never more applicable than in thinking through lead definitions. Despite what you hear from some "experts," there is not and should not be a universal definition of a qualified lead. There is too much variability in organizations and their sales cycles for that.

Let's explore some of the variables that impact the definition of a qualified lead. How you define a lead depends on:

- What you are selling and who you are selling to
- Your sales cycle times and average deal size
- If the field sales team is hunters/farmers or only hunters
- The sizes of the teams who qualify leads, do outbound prospecting, and carry quotas
- The number of initial leads (aka inquiries) that marketing generates
- The number of highly scored sales ready leads that marketing generates
- The gap to quota faced by the individual sales rep

Before we get into how these variables affect your lead definition, we first need to revisit our old friend BANT.

The acronym BANT (Budget, Authority, Need, Timing) is used by many organizations to gauge the degree of qualification of a lead. There are many debates over the efficacy of BANT in the modern selling environment. Google 'BANT is dead' to see for yourself. And the debates make sense. In many cases buyers no longer have pre-defined projects with set budgets and timeframes. Asking a team of SDRs to BANT qualify every inquiry that marketing passes their way means that the sales team probably won't get a lot of leads.

My friend Ken Krogue, founder of InsideSales.com, proposes a new acronym called ANUM (Authority, Need, Urgency, Money) to address this. I personally love it. The subtle difference is that absent projects, marketing and sales teams need to create demand higher within the organization. You need to start by building need with the authority figures in a prospect account. Only once you have authority and need can you build urgency and help them figure out how they are going to fund it. This subtle difference between project based solution selling and challenger based consultative selling has been proven empirically by the research team at the Corporate Executive Board (my former employer). Buy the book *The Challenger Sale* by my friends Brent Adamson and Matt Dixon for more on this.

Keep ANUM in the back of your mind as we return to the definition of a qualified lead.

Think of the lead hand off from marketing (or SDRs) to sales as light passing through the lens of a camera. If you open the aperture wide, more light passes through. You might want to do this on a darker day or in the evening when there is less light. If you close the aperture, less light passes through. You might want to do this on a bright sunny day or indoors to avoid over-exposing the picture.

The degree to which you open or close the aperture depends on how many leads the organization needs to thrive. Adding or removing a letter from ANUM becomes a great way to dynamically adjust this.

Here is a spectrum of options when it comes to lead definitions. On the left side of the spectrum you see a wide open aperture. This organization has decided to define a qualified lead as a meeting with the right person at the right account that meets our ideal customer profile (ICP). The only variable present from ANUM is the A for Authority.

Organizations might use a loose lead definition if they:

- Are far behind quota
- Have few SDRs
- Have sales teams who only hunt
- Have few inquiries through marketing
- Sell to senior people at larger organizations who don't come inbound

- Have an evangelical product that is still unknown by the market

The goal for this aperture position is to let a lot of leads through and give the sales team lots of 'at bats' to build their opportunity pipelines. A strategy would be to do more outbound prospecting to find people who meet this definition of a qualified lead.

On the other end of the spectrum you see a mostly closed aperture. This organization has decided to define a qualified lead as meeting with the right person at the right account that meets our ICP *as well as* having a specific need, urgency to take action, and an understanding of the source of money to fund the purchase. All of the variables of ANUM are present: Authority, Need, Urgency, and Money.

Organizations might use a tight lead definition if they:

- Have a lot of SDRs
- Have sales teams who hunt/farm and are too busy for new opportunities
- Have a lot of inquiries through marketing
- Sell to junior people at smaller companies who more readily come inbound
- Have a hot offering that is creating pull demand

The goal for this aperture position is to only pass the most highly qualified leads. This keeps the sales team focused on the best deals. A strategy would be to stop doing outbound prospecting and instead rely on marketing automation software like Eloqua, Marketo, Pardot, HubSpot, Silverpop, etc. to do system-automated lead qualification and scoring.

Most organizations pick something in the middle of the two extremes. Clients of Vorsight's outsourced appointment setting service typically receive meetings with the right person from the right target account with interest and, in some cases, specific needs. Our BDAs (same as SDRs) do their best to identify urgency and money as well. These are difficult to establish when outbound prospecting. Put yourself in the shoes of the executive being called out of the blue. Would you be willing to answer questions about budget when 2 minutes ago you didn't even know this solution existed? It's like going to a bar, meeting a girl, and asking her to marry you before the first date. It's possible, but highly unlikely.

There are dangers with each approach as well. If you open the aperture too wide you will flood the sales team with <u>Fool's Gold</u>. They will waste a lot of time qualifying. If you close the aperture too narrow you will lose out on opportunities with people in active buying cycles who get frustrated in the lack of a human response. Corporate decision makers increasingly tune out drip email nurture streams from marketing automation. While you wait for the lead to score high enough to call, they have already selected another vendor.

The B2B sales and marketing analysts from <u>SiriusDecisions</u> tell us that a balanced mix of inbound and outbound is always present in healthy sales funnels. This may be counter-intuitive to the "cold calling is dead" crowd, but the SD research to back it up is very clear.

I hope this helps as you think through the right definition of a qualified lead for your organization.

How do you define a qualified lead?

Sales Hack contributed by: Steve Richard, CRO, ExecVision.io & Founder, VorsightBP

Steve is a student of buying / selling and learn something new every day.

Steve's passion and life's work is to fix the top of the sales funnel —prospecting, lead qualification, and social selling—for sales reps and managers. Whereas most sales organizations have a good process for taking qualified sales appointments to close, most do not have a repeatable and scalable process for getting those opportunities started.

Sales training companies neglect this problem by presuming you have an appointment or opportunity in the first place. What if you don't? VorsightBP's mission is to bring research, science, and real data to help solve the problem for our clients.

SALES HACK #5
GIVE YOUR SALES FORCE FEWER LEADS

Too many raw, unqualified leads can create a clogged marketing and sales process and an unhealthy sales funnel.

Want to fully leverage the talents of your sales force?

Then stop expecting sales reps to filter leads, qualify them, and then cultivate the long-term ones until they are ready buyers. They just won't do it. Why? Because they are compensated—and rightly so—to focus on making the immediate numbers, not on building a pipeline of prospects.

But if not sales, then who? Marketing? No. Let's face it, most marketing departments are not built to nurture leads. That's not their purpose. They are filled with brand builders and communicators who do not possess lead management skills and technology, or they are measured on "response rates" and so-called "cost-per-lead," which are the wrong metrics.

Instead, a separate group, inside or outside the company, needs to take control of the incredibly vital function of lead development. Think of this group as "lead farmers," or prospect development specialists who do the following:

- Qualify raw leads;
- Nurture lukewarm prospects into the hot category;
- Turn the developed leads over to the sales force for harvesting.

Often this process takes months. But it's worth it because a developed lead is one that sets the stage for relationship selling. A lead farmer equips the sales rep with in-depth knowledge about the prospect, such as insight into the prospect's motivations, pain points and buying plans. Armed with this knowledge, Sales Hack can engage the prospect in a consultative conversation rather than launching into a cold-call presentation or a discovery interview.

But what about marketing automation?

Good question. Despite its popularity, the marketing automation used to manage inbound leads is not equipped to filter and/or prequalify leads. In fact, thanks to automation, marketing is able to send more unqualified leads to sales faster than ever before.

Contrary to popular belief, sales reps don't need more leads. They need fewer leads—or more accurately, fewer raw, unfiltered, unqualified leads. Sales reps need leads that have been carefully qualified, properly and consistently nurtured and appropriately developed, increasing the likelihood of a completed sale.

A sales exec recently told me he would "rather have 10% of my current lead flow with 80% of the leads being high quality than the current state of affairs where only 5% of leads are qualified, at best."

When sales reps get bombarded with unqualified leads they become conditioned to distrust all leads. When they realize the leads are simply based on form completions regardless of need or fit, they don't bother following up. What competent Sales Hack is willing to expend precious time and resources to cull through a hundred leads to find five good ones?

So instead, they resort to generating their own leads. In average companies, sales must find 60% or more of the leads they need to make their numbers, according to Marketo. While some best-in-class organizations have reduced the percentage to 38%, this number is still too high. Sales Hack should be closing deals, not generating, qualifying and nurturing leads.

The true measure of success

- Marketing should be judged by how well it creates sales opportunities that have a high potential of developing into sales.
- Sales should be evaluated on how well they close these good leads from marketing.

Far too many companies, however, evaluate marketing's success by the number of leads they hand over to sales. These companies do not have effective processes and methodologies to track anything other than the number of leads generated and their cost.

Many of the same companies fail to hold sales accountable for closing the good leads and for reporting back results that feed the marketing and sales model. The overall result is often wasted marketing dollars and wasted sales time.

Nurturing is Key - *Nurturing is essential for successful lead* *generation—both inbound and outbound. In fact, I propose that nurturing is the most underutilized marketing activity.*

Additional contact using multiple touches via multiple media—including phone, voicemail and email—across multiple cycles is well worth the time and expense.

Generally speaking, nurturing programs increase the lead rate significantly.

- Standard lead-generation programs produce an average 5% lead rate.
- Advanced lead-generation programs (which include nurturing) produce an average 15% lead rate—a whopping three times higher.

Clearly, the "lead farming" role is incompatible with the sales role. Good prospect developers are hard to find. The best approach to performing the job effectively is to:

- Assign it to a specialized in-house team with no direct sales responsibility.
- Outsource it to a firm totally focused on nurturing leads into sales opportunities.

By not passing unfiltered, unqualified leads to your sales team—and focusing instead on delivering fewer, yet more qualified prospects—you have the very real potential to significantly impact your organization's ability to generate revenue.

Sales Hack contributed by: Dan McDade, President & CEO, PointClear

Dan McDade founded PointClear in 1997 to help B2B companies with complex sales processes drive more revenue through effective lead generation, qualification and nurturing. For more than 15 years, he's been instrumental in developing innovative strategies that assure 100% of leads delivered to client sales organizations are fully qualified to client specifications—enabling them to close up to 5 times more deals.

Dan is the author of *The Truth About Leads*, an insightful book that sheds light on little-known

secrets that help focus B2B lead-generation efforts, align sales and marketing organizations, and drive revenue. He also wrote *From Chaos to Kickass*, an ebook detailing benefits of sales and marketing optimization that received a silver award from Top Sales World; and he authors ViewPoint | The Truth About Lead Generation, a blog exploring issues related to B2B sales, marketing and lead generation.

SALES HACK #6
START EVERY SALES CALL WITH THESE TWO QUESTIONS

Artful Discovery involves more than simply gathering requirements. Instead, Discovery should represent a collaborative process where we help expand our knowledge about the prospect's Need, Buying Process, and Desired Results

Personally, I consider Discovery to be the most important part of the sales process because it establishes a context in which we can add real value. I wanted to share with you one of my very simple (but very important) techniques.

The two most important questions you can ask in any discovery conversation, particularly if you are bridging from a previous discovery conversation, are:

1) What do you recall (or what stands out?) from our last conversation?

2) What is new and different in your world since we last spoke?

When I ask a prospect what stands out from our last conversation, I am acknowledging I am only a small part of their world. As such, they may or may not remember a lot about our last conversation. Knowing exactly what they recall helps me bridge the conversation. That is, pick up in the right place or fill in the gaps.

It is important to anchor the conversation we are having now using their perception of the previous meeting rather than our own.

The second question is important because selling implies dealing with a situation in constant motion. Your prospect has not been sitting at their desk staring into space and pondering what you discussed last week. They have been living life. Perhaps they have experienced changes in their personal life. They certainly have experienced change in their professional role. It's important to know these things.

On occasion, I have found out late in a conversation that the contact I have been working with has been moved (or will be moving) to a new role. Trust me - this is something you want to learn in the first five minutes of the conversation rather than after you've presented for an hour and a half. I've also uncovered positive information such as an upcoming promotion or the existence of a new corporate mandate aligned with my solution.

The point is this. Selling is a profession of service. We must understand our prospect's environment completely in order to serve them effectively. Placing their perspective at the front of the conversation demonstrates a respect for them that will differentiate you from the hoard of vendors simply waiting for their turn to speak.

Sales Hack contributed by: Townsend Wardlaw, Sales Speaker, Trainer, and Blogger (www.townsendwardlaw.com)

Townsend Wardlaw's boutique consultancy works with Founders and CEO's of companies earning between $1M and $10M to help them drive

real and sustainable change within their sales organizations.

As a trusted advisor that guides companies to double revenue over the following 18 - 24 months, he has the unique ability to translate complex concepts into a prioritized and executable roadmap based on documented and repeatable processes.

Most importantly, he is passionate about rolling up his sleeves to launch or transform a sales organization!

SALES HACK #7
TWO RULES FOR SELLING TO HUMANS

Robin Dreeke is an FBI veteran. He previously led the Behavioral Analysis Program for the FBI and studied the science behind relationship development for over 27 years.

In his recent book, *It's Not All About "Me"*, he shares this simple advice:

Suspend your ego to get people to like you.

Suspending your ego means putting what you want, what your company wants, and what you're compensated for aside for a moment. It is about breaking down the natural resistance that prospects exhibit when being contacted by *a seller*. It is also damn difficult to do.

As a hard-charging Sales Development Rep, this probably goes against your instincts. After all, you're paid to break into accounts and instigate change.

But as the title of this chapter suggests, you make that job a lot harder when you swim against the current of human behavior. There's a well-worn Dale Carnegie line from *How to Win Friend and Influence People*. It goes, "You can make more friends in two months by becoming interested in other people than you can in two years by trying to get other people interested in you."

But 99.9% of sales development reps ignore this advice. The overwhelming majority of reps calling on your prospects are using *self-centric, ego-filled* messaging. Here's what that sounds like:

"I'd love to chat with you about your sales strategies…."

 "I wanted to drop a quick note to see if you had the chance to review my email from a few days ago."

"If you are not the right person, I would appreciate if you can point me to the right contact."

I have two rules and a few examples I'd like to share. They will help you launch into the elite 1% of sellers *who understand human behavior and don't try to fight it.*

SELLING TO HUMANS Rule #1: Be Interested OR BE IGNORED

No one is listening to you. Prospects are just too busy. Before you can convince them to care about what you're saying, you have to get to them to actually hear you.

Average sales messaging fails miserably at this. It just doesn't stand out. Average messaging sounds like this:

> *Hi John, Guy Sellers here with SomeSoft . I was just hoping to get 30 minutes on your calendar to discuss your [INSERT] strategy. You can reach me at....*

Or this:

> *John,*
>
> *Guy with SomeSoft. I hope you're doing well. I saw that you had downloaded some information on our tool a while back. I wanted to reach out and see if you had any follow up questions.*
>
> *I'd be happy to take you through a high-level overview of our solution. What does your schedule look like this week?*

These types of message are pure ego.

There's no attempt to customize, offer value, or show interest in the individual prospect. Every prospect worth calling gets dozens of messages like these daily. And they all respond the same way: DELETE.

Ben Haines is the Chief Information Officer of Pabst Brewing Company. In an interview with ZDnet, he shared the following.

> *"99% of the calls [I receive] are, 'I'd like to know what your IT strategy is and how we can help you.' I just delete those."*

If you want prospects to care, you have to get them to listen. If you want them to listen, you have to first show you're interested. You have to suspend your ego.

One way to do this is to demonstrate relevancy. For example, you could reference something happening in their industry, with their role, at their company, or something they shared in an interview or on Twitter/LinkedIn.

Think of it this way. If you turn on the news and they're discussing a storm in a neighboring state, you may or may not pay any attention. If you turn on the news and they're discussing a storm in *your city*, you'll devote your full attention. The same holds true for your prospects. *What one little thing about this person can you put in your message that will make them tune in?*

OK, on to a few real-world examples (both good and bad).

Consider the following example:

> *Hi Dana, Pat Smith here from SomeSoft. 555.432.1212. Wanted to reach out to and just follow up on an email I had sent you last week. Hopefully you had a chance to take a look at it and found the information interesting….*

That preamble took 16 seconds and said absolutely nothing. Compare that to the following:

> *Hi Dana, I'm calling today to share a research report we just published on Sales Rep retention trends. In it we identify three strategies that can decrease rep attrition by 50%. This is Pat Smith at SomeSoft. To receive your copy, you can reach me at 555.432.1212.*

Now that entire message took about 22 seconds to deliver. It is relevant, offers something of value, and comes in under 30 seconds. Boom!

An SVP of Sales at a B2B technology company forwarded me this voicemail. As you read it, note when you would have hit delete.

> *Good afternoon Dana. This is Pat Smith over at SomeSoft. I'm the Corporate Account Manager here. My direct line is 555.432.1212. I was reaching out to you today, I had something come across my desk that you had attended a webinar late last year in regards to looking at our application over at your company. Wanted to one, get in touch, introduce myself. I am one of two account managers that work on your account. In addition, I wanted to understand a little bit better possibly about some needs coming up this year and, if possible, if you wanted to get some more time with one of our Client Executives. Definitely love to get you in touch with them. If you have some time, we can set up a time here later this week or early next. My direct line is 555.432.1212. Thanks and have a great day.*

Would any part of that message get a prospect to really stop and listen? I don't think so.

The sad part is that poor sucker shows up every day and work his buns off leaving those messages.

SELLING TO HUMANS
Rule #2: Be Specific OR BE IGNORED

Humans are inherently lazy.

People substitute hard questions for easy ones. The easiest question of all is *"Can I ignore this?"*

If your calls-to-action are too vague, too broad, or too complex, you're handing prospects a perfect excuse to ignore your message. You have to ask for something very specific if you have any hope of receiving a reply.

Strong calls-to-action sound like:
- *To receive your copy of the [insert very relevant topic] research, you can reach me at… <offer of research>*
- *I don't want to miss your call so here's my mobile number is… <you're important enough to have my personal number>*

Weak ones are similar to:
- *You downloaded our ebook and I wanted to see if you have any questions…. <could you be more boring?>*
- *Wanted to see if there are synergies between our companies. My number is…. <what does that even mean?! >*

Do you see the difference?

Small and direct calls-to-action, high responses. Big and unclear calls-to-action, low responses. This is just how we humans are wired.

I hope you can see that I'm not suggesting you blow up the way you're messaging prospects today. I am suggesting that you reevaluate what you're doing by keeping Rule #1 and Rule #2 in mind.

Sales development is important work and what you do matters. Good selling and keep hacking!

(Note: This is an excerpt from Trish's upcoming book on Sales Development due out in Q1 2016.)

Sales Hack contributed by: Trish Bertuzzi, Queen of Inside sales

So, okay, the title is one she gave herself but Trish had been in the B2B Inside Sales game for over 25 years. She is the Founder and CEO of The

Bridge Group, Inc. and her firm works with technology companies helping them to unleash the power of Inside Sales. Trish has been featured in Forbes as well as Inc. Magazine and has received the Lifetime Achievement Award from the American Association of Inside Sales Professionals.

SALES HACK #8
LEVERAGE LIVE BODIES

If you're in acquisition sales or Business Development, you're likely working the numbers, right? You have a lead list or territory of a few hundred, and we just need a few of these babies to pop to start making the dough. So this hack is about NOT giving all accounts the same attention or calling your list alphabetically (gasp!), but instead getting smart about categorizing your work. I call it "win fast lose fast" and we'll do it by *leveraging live bodies*.

That means calling at the front door and leveraging anyone we can get to talk to us to quickly qualify the account. Then we can sort the list and work the "A" leads 10x harder than the crap on the bottom.

Step one: *Don't* call the Decision Maker. What? Really, unless you're using ConnectAndSell, you're not going to get him anyway, so why waste all day leaving voicemails? Instead go on a reconnaissance effort. Think James Bond or Jason Bourne: Get in, get your info, try not to leave too much collateral damage, but don't get out until you get what you need.

Step two: Create the "get" list. Most companies can be qualified enough to sort into ABCD piles with three basic pieces of information: company size, what they do or industry, and common activities or trends. The key is to make these simple enough that anyone can answer them (so no, their budget for SaaS upgrades doesn't fit the bill here).

Step three: Get "lost" in the phone system and wind up in the sales, service, or accounting departments or with a gatekeeper (stay away from IT and HR: voicemail central). Now ask for help and hit them hard and fast with three to five questions. Sure they'll wonder who the hell you are and will probably ask that by question four, but would Jason Bourne care? Ruffle a few feathers; you don't have to have them over to dinner and they won't remember who you are anyway! (OK, modify this for tiny accounts).

Example: A Fortune 500 technology company had a team selling printers to small businesses. The list was pretty poor - literally dialing 100 times to talk to one decision maker, and then finding out they had like 1 printer and it was replenished last year. Not a lot of future opportunity here right?

Here's the fix:

Sales Hack Rep: *Hi, this is LB from Factor 8 and I seriously need your help. I have a meeting with IT tomorrow, and I've been lost in your phone system trying to get ahold of my guy. Help me out would you? (1) Tell me, how many people work there at ABC Company? (2) Do you all do work on computers? (3) Do you have your own printer or do you have to share it? (3b)With how many people? (4)Did you get a new one in the last few years?*

Right about now they'll start to waver and hit you with something like, "Um, who did you say you were looking for again?" Don't sweat it. In fact, the masters will answer, build a little rapport and go in for another 3-5 questions about the account (is this your only location?), the competition (what kind of printer do you have?) and even the contact (do you know Mr. Decision Maker?).

Now I know that this account has three people and one printer . . . or 300 people and 10 old printers. Which one am I going to work harder to call?

Tip: Note the conversational tone of my questions. Also note that I didn't ask complex questions. Believe me, this works 200X better than asking, "How many PC's and Printers are in your office?" Instant shut-down!

Try splitting your day into reconnaissance missions and Decision Maker hunting, and for once you might even enjoy the fact that you aren't getting anyone on the phone! Happy Hunting!

Sales Hack contributed by: Lauren Bailey, President, Factor 8

Voted "Top 25 Most Influential Leaders in Inside Sales" by The American Association of Inside Sales Professionals 2013 and 2014. President of Factor 8, 2014 award-winner for Inside Sales and Leadership Training.

After spending nearly 20 years launching and leading Inside Sales organizations around the World, Factor 8 President Lauren Bailey has put her dual background in sales and training leadership to work for companies launching, scaling, and optimizing Inside Sales teams. She's worked with IBM, SAP, Ingram Micro, Microsoft, Grainger, HP, Staples, and many more. Often brought in to benchmark Inside Sales Organizations, Lauren and her team help Sales Leaders see where they stack up against the Best in Class of Inside Sales, and build roadmaps to meet goals, scale, and exceed quotas.

SALES HACK #9
SELLING BELOW THE SURFACE, BEYOND THE FEAR

There are many things that people will argue are the demise of a sales opportunity. However many of those things are not always within the sales rep's control. Of the things that a sales rep can control there are two that stand out the most. Interestingly, they go hand-in-hand; in fact, one begets the next. The two most dominating forces within a sales rep's control are fear and their ability to go beyond the surface pains of their prospects.

Imagine you are VP of Sales for a SaaS company that sells to corporations with over 1,000 employees. Your sales cycle is 6-12 months and the average deal size is $120k ARR.

On June 20th, your sales rep tells you that s/he has a deal that they expect to close before the end of the quarter. On June 27, 28, and 29 your rep keeps telling you the deal is still expected to close. Then comes June 30, and what happens? The deal doesn't close.

As a VP you are furious. You committed the revenue to the CEO who in turn committed it to the board. You trusted your sales rep. You trusted the prospect. You trusted your sales process. So what happened?

This happens everywhere, at every company, and to every Vice President of Sales we know. Why does it happen? And more importantly what can be done to make it stop?

There are two very important pieces to this puzzle that a VP of Sales and Sales Rep can control.

1. Better Discovery = Going beyond the Surface Pains.
2. Controlling Fear = Accept that asking the questions you are afraid to ask is actually better for everyone, including the prospect.

Surface Pain Selling (aka – Features & Benefits Selling)

Surface Pains are those pains that a prospect will tell the sales person that makes the sales person "think" a deal is imminent, but in reality are merely a smokescreen that will distract the sales person. In many cases the prospect themselves do not even realize they are only providing surface pains. The most prominent symptom of surface pains is something we call "Happy Ears".

Happy Ears occur when a sales rep hears what they want to hear, but does not dig deeper to uncover the pains below the surface. It means taking the prospects comments only at face value and not professionally questioning beyond that value. The surest examples of this occur when a sales rep moves to demo and focuses on features and benefits of the products.

In sales there are surface pains and core pains; however, in order to get to the core pains a sales rep must become part doctor, part detective, part journalist, and part psychiatrist. We will pick this up again but note - a sales rep is NEVER a mind reader.

Go back to your old science class when you were studying the earth. If you don't recall, the earth has several layers: The Surface, the Mantle, and the Core. In sales, just like the earth, the core is where it all begins.

So, how do we get to the core? Well most sales people understand they need to ask questions. Unfortunately most sales people do not understand the types of questions to ask and just as important the types of follow-up questions they need to ask.

In order to close any sale there are 3 questions that must be answered, ALWAYS!

1. **What** is the pain that needs to be solved?
2. **Why** is solving this pain important to the decision maker and the organization?
3. **How** does this solving this pain impact the decision maker and the organization?

In many cases the "What" or "Surface Pain" are really not even pains; in fact they are symptoms of a deeper issue. Let's say you've had a cough for a week. It hurts to cough, your body aches, your throat is sore and you have a low grade fever. Finally you take all of this information and you go to the doctor. The doctor now has to decide what is really wrong with you. Is it a cold? Is it a flu? Do you have bronchitis? Do you have emphysema?

What we now understand is that your cough, pains, and fever, while painful, are not the real issue. In fact they are symptoms, not the disease.

This is the same thing a sales rep must understand and work towards solving. By focusing merely on the surface pains the sales rep is really just giving the prospect over the counter remedies like Tylenol to treat the symptoms when they should be asking more to see if a prescription for antibiotics is what's needed.

It's been our experience that sales reps are great at getting to surface pains. In fact most first meetings are set based on a certain level of surface pain exposure or discovery (symptoms). The problem is that most reps either don't know how to go deeper to get to the core pains or they are afraid.

Here's another example. Let's say you and your wife have been invited to a very fancy fundraiser where there is a good chance for both of you to do some networking that can advance a cause you both support very deeply. Here's the challenge: it's Monday, and you just got the invite. The party is Friday night. Your wife decides she wants to go out and buy a new dress, which you support. Unfortunately there is not enough time for her to try on the dress so she picks one out not knowing if it will fit and brings it home.

Fast forward to Friday 5pm. She tries it on. You truly think she looks awesome, but she looks at herself in the mirror, turns around one way, looks up and down, turns around the other way, looks up and down again. She then asks you what you think, you tell her she looks beautiful. So she goes back to the mirror and does another set of turns and looks from every direction. Then she lets out a big sigh and says something like "Nope, can't wear this, I look awful."

Then she decides to wear her "Go to Black Dress".

So what happened exactly? Well, unfortunately it was a purchase that was made solely on a "what" question. Here's what we mean, and yes, we've been through this not only with our spouses but also with our own purchases.

What is the pain that needs solving? – There's an important event coming and your significant other needs something new to wear.

Why is it important to solve this pain of having a new dress? – Because this cause is important to both of you she wants to put her best foot forward.

How does having a new dress affect her and the important cause? While it is important she thinks she looks good in the dress, more importantly she wants to "feel good" in the dress. If she doesn't feel good then it will not matter how you or anyone else thinks she looks.

So this is the exact same thing your prospects must go through. They not only want to solve their pain based on your solution, but they also want to feel good about the purchase. In other words, do not treat the symptoms, cure the disease.

The purchase is important to them. In many cases the "How it affects them" is twofold. First, it will mean something significant to the organization they are representing, similar to that cause that was so important to you. If what you offer helps their organization become more profitable, drive more revenue or solve another significant pain, the company will be happy. If the product or service does all of these things, then your prospect, the one who made the decision to purchase your products or services, will be seen positively throughout the organization. His or her career should benefit from the success you helped them to achieve.

Now you cannot simply walk into a sales meeting and start asking "What? Why? How?" every time you discover a surface pain. In fact there are tons of sales techniques one can use. The simplest explanation is knowing that the answer to "How?" is always based on the answer behind the first answer or the question behind the question. (Remember when we talked about being part journalist?) It's something that can be learned and unfortunately is not often taught these days. It's not the first question you ask, but the follow up question on the same subject matter that gets you closer to the core.

The Fear Factory

So why are sales reps not doing this? Aside from not being taught, they are most often afraid. You see, they get to surface pains, then they get happy ears, and then make assumptions based on the features and benefits of your solution. They lump every pain of every prospect into the same bucket. When they hear the prospect get excited about your feature set the euphoria and endorphin rush they feel is real. They "feel" like they are in a good place in the sales cycle, the "feel" like they have rapport with the prospect. They "feel" they have uncovered a real opportunity. In reality, they have nothing. No real rapport with the customer, no real understanding of their challenges, and no real opportunity to put in the pipeline. The Sales Rep thinks that because each prospect has "Surface Pain 1" that all prospects experience the same surface pain the same way and therefore the same solution will work for everyone.

Go back to the coughing example. It's very possible for two people to live in the same house, have the same cough, and the same fever. However it's also very possible one person just has a cold and the other person has Strep Throat, which means that how you treat each person will be completely different from the other.

Sadly what is often the case is that the sales rep is afraid to ask more questions. They are afraid they might ask something "too personal." They are afraid they might "offend" the prospect. They are afraid to ask about the competition because they think it will put an idea into the prospects mind to go and seek out the competitor.

Imagine if you went to your doctor with this bad cough. How would you feel if s/he did not ask questions about your daily habits, such as smoking? Or exercise? Would you trust your doctor? Don't you expect your doctor to ask you questions that may make you feel a bit uncomfortable even if you appear healthy?

In the sales world we call this fear "The Fear Factory" ©. "The Fear Factory"© churns out excuses 24/7 for sales reps. The Fear Factory © always highlights the worst case scenarios. The Fear Factory © is part of the mental game for sales reps. Often times it's driven by a single experience, a worst case scenario, an outlier, and often sounds like this, "well there was this one time when…" Furthermore, The Fear Factory © in some cases is the root cause of a cancer within the sales organization. It's the one rep who loves to share their misery with the rest of the team that brings everyone down. Fortunately, this type of cancer is treatable and can be sent into remission in various ways as long as the sales leaders are willing to do their jobs.

When you have been in sales as long as we have you know that the combination of "Surface Pain Selling" and "The Fear Factory" create a ton of toxic waste. The amount of sludge, slime, and ooze produced creates a gummy and messy pipeline. It creates a revenue forecast that is so bloated it's just not believable. It will have short term consequences and long term effects on the overall health of the organization.

Respect Contracts© & Mini-Contracts©

So how do you solve these issues from not drilling down to the core pain? How do take the fear away from the reps and make them strong again? Well it all starts in the beginning. You can no more easily tell someone to just ask better questions than you can just hand someone three tennis balls and tell them to start juggling. Likewise, you cannot just tell someone to stop being afraid to ask questions just like you cannot just go out and run a full marathon tomorrow without putting in any training.

So where do you begin? Well that's easy. You begin where everything begins; at the beginning of course. And it all begins with one word, RESPECT. Sales reps must not only respect their prospects, but they have to respect themselves. Sales reps must give themselves permission to earn the right to ask questions of their prospect. Sales reps need to get permission and agreement from prospects that both parties are going to ask questions of each other. Finally, sales reps must be willing to "fire" the prospect if it's not a right fit.

This should happen continually through the sales process but it must occur immediately in the first Qualification and/or Discovery Call. Most reps we work with these days do not understand how to run a sales call. They take no control, they offer weak professional introductions and do not understand how to lay out the foundation for the discussion. They do not understand the purpose of the call as compared with the agenda of the call. They often times fumble and stumble through introductions, and then just try to rush right into a demo; or even worse, just answer the prospect's questions and then go straight into the demo.

So what is a "Respect Contract"©, and what does it look like? A "Respect Contract"© is a verbal agreement between two parties that sets the stage and lays the ground rules of engagement—not just the first meeting but for every subsequent meeting after that. It will level the playing field. It will earn and confirm the respect each party has for one another and allow either party to end the engagement without it being misinterpreted as personal.

A great "Respect Contract"© consists of things like Introductions, Time, Purpose, Agenda, Outcomes. It psychologically tells the prospect they have control when in fact it gives all of the control to the sales rep. In short the sales rep is giving the prospect the "It's not you, it's me" speech.

Here's an example.

- **Time** – Confirm the time commitment with the parties, ask for hard stops. (Remember your time is as valuable as theirs)

- **Introductions** – The rep asks everyone in the meeting to give a quick intro, their title, and what they want to achieve from the discussion. (Tedious, yes, but critical to earning respect and learning surface pains without asking a ton of questions).

- **Purpose** – The rep defines this with something like... "The purpose of our call today is to create a mutual frame of reference about the challenges ABC Company is facing and where we may be able to help you. In order to do this I want the lines of communication to be a two-way street where we both ask questions and ask for clarification if something seems too vague."

- **Agenda** – The rep defines the agenda with 3 bullet points and asks if anyone has something they want to add?

- **Outcomes** – The rep says something like, "We suspect one of two things will happen at the end of this call; either we will schedule another call with all interested parties, or one of us is going to decide this isn't the right fit for them."

- **Mini-Agreement** – The rep says something like, "So if this all sounds good to you I'd like to proceed. By the way, if you ever feel like we aren't the right fit, please tell me and likewise if I cannot help you I will do the same. We both value our time and the last thing I want to do is waste either of ours. Additionally I don't want to chase you down with annoying emails and phone calls. How does that sound?"

Conclusion

There are so many tools in the market today to help sales reps do their jobs. While the prospect is now able to have more information about vendors than ever before the playing field is still equal as the rep is now able to have more information about their prospect than ever before too. On top of this information there are tons of tools to help a sales rep gather this information and gain greater insight into the minds of prospects and truly understand the companies they are selling into. The one thing that still has not changed even with all this new technology is the fact that a sales deal must still involve a conversation by at least two people.

What used to be called the "It Factor" or "Secret Sauce" in defining great sales reps is not really a secret. It's actually something that can now be seen, heard, and addressed directly with every sales rep within the organization. Yes, there are definitely personality and psychological make-ups that lend themselves to the sales persona; however you can now make sure your sales reps know what to look and listen for in their sales calls. The end result will be a stronger pipeline with fewer leaks, and a forecast that will become more and more accurate over time.

If you have any questions please feel free to reach out to us directly at richard@theharrisconsultinggroup.com or follow us on Twitter: @rharris415 and @saasselling.

Sales Hack contributed by: Richard Harris, Owner, The Harris Consulting Group

Awarded AA-ISP's TOP 25 Most Influential Inside Sales Professionals in 2015.

Richard is a seasoned SaaS sales leader and trainer with 20+ years experience helping early stage and expansion stage start-ups build their sales infrastructure and train their sales teams to "get there faster". Clients include: Gainsight, LevelEleven, Workspot, Spanning, and TopOpps.

SALES HACK #10
CALLING HIGH IS NOT THE TRICK: THE TRICK IS WHEN YOU ARE THERE WHAT DO YOU SAY

<u>The Story</u>

Gary knew something was wrong. Jim, the manager of IT Services, has not called back in three days. He didn't answer an email, and didn't return a couple of voice messages. Sure, the decision was not supposed to be made until this coming Friday, two days from now, but it just seemed odd, since Gary has talked with Jim almost daily over the past two weeks.

The deal had gone quite well over the past 60 days. It started with Jim calling in to Gary's company and having in interest in their product. They talked a bit, had a really good discussion about what Jim was looking for, and mutually came to a conclusion that there was a good reason to keep the discussion going.

The Discovery phase went well, and Jim discussed his decision criteria. Gary was even able to add some decision criteria items Jim thought were important and didn't know he could get. It seemed like Gary and Jim were working well together.

A WebEx meeting went great with Susan, Jim's boss and the VP of IT. She asked a few questions, and was really pleasant at the end. She assured Gary that Jim was the decision maker for this solution.

All throughout the final demo and the proposal phase, Jim seemed to like all the options Gary was offering. The proposal was a mutually developed document and Jim expressed to Gary how thorough and complete the process had been. That was three days ago, and with two days left until decision day it seemed odd that Jim would go "dark", but Gary convinced himself that all vendors were probably shut out in these final days so the prospect could make a decision. After all, it's a $200,000 decision, and one that shouldn't be taken lightly. Long story short, Gary will probably not get this deal. Could be a few reasons:

- The competition knew a C-Level executive in the prospect's organization.
- The competition dropped its price and presented a killer offer.
- Jim was overruled by Susan or someone else.

There is a lot that can happen that will cause a sales person to lose a deal at the last minute. Surprises at the end of a sale rarely turn out to be good.

Two Value Propositions

We hear about these deals all the time, and in a good majority of them, what Gary didn't do was to get both value propositions on this deal. That's right, every deal has _two_ value propositions, and if Gary only gets one, in this case Jim's, he is running a big risk of losing this deal, or at worst, not getting all the value for his offering, and he will be forced to discount to get the deal.

Welcome to the land of two value propositions for every deal; welcome to selling above and below the line.

Selling Above and Below the Line - ATL/BTL

Salespeople are a pretty robotic lot. They join a company, sit through training, learn about the product or service they are selling, and then go at it. It's a war.

You have to battle the competition, get though executive screens, handle objections, and get around buyers who do not see the benefit of what you are selling to win a deal. It's a fast paced career, and with a monthly quota hanging over a salesperson's head, there is really no room for mistakes, and definitely no room to hide.

Companies go to great lengths to make sure salespeople are ready for this spirited battle. They give them trained technical service people so they don't have to spend all their time dealing with the technical questions of what they are selling. They also and give them discount authority so they can match any "foolish" competitive offer. Companies want salespeople focusing on the bigger picture; getting the sale.

What salespeople are coached to do

Of course, when the salesperson starts selling, and develops a pipeline of deals, sales management starts "coaching":

These would be typical coaching questions, and are usually focused on the deal and what will it take to get the deal in.

> "What will it take to get this deal in?"
>
> "How well is the competition doing?"
>
> "Where are we strong and where are we weak based on their needs?"

How business buys

Of course, this coaching process the manager is engaging in is very different than the process of how businesses buy. Most companies really don't care about all the things that sales organizations do. What they care about is getting answers to their problems. Which leads to the two main differences between the seller's and the buyer's processes.

1. Companies buy in stages, not in deals. They have a process of how they buy that is different that the sales process managers are coaching to.
2. Companies have two value propositions for any purchase, and most salespeople are trained and coached to go after only one.

Stages

We now know that there is a buying process that companies go though. It really doesn't matter what number of stages that the buyer and seller claim they go through; it just matters that there is a buying process companies follow, and salespeople must pattern their selling process after their prospect's buying process.

Sales organizations are doing this more and more. Sales managers are now looking at stages in deals and trying to mimic the buyer's stages with their selling stages, all with varying degrees of success. They usually start out with a sales process. Typical steps in this sales process are:

1. Initial/Plan
2. Discovery
3. Demonstration/Align
4. Propose/Negotiations

5. Close

Typical Sales Process

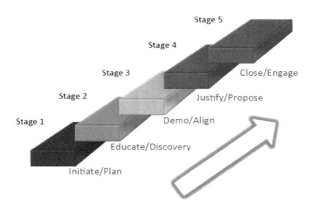

Notice this approach focuses the sales team on the process and steps of the sale, not just the final outcome. For too long sales management has focused and coached on the final decision (Close) and not the process. This new "stage" focus is a good first attempt.

Cause

However, what is missing at a deeper level is what is really going on with the buyer. What is causing the buyer to make an investment? What is causing the executives of the company to spend time, effort and resources on something? What's going on?

What is going on in the prospect's world is change. Something is causing a change within the organization. What is it?

The Hunt for Two Value Propositions

So now there are two value propositions the sales team must uncover. Salespeople need to understand what is:

1. Causing the organization to change, as well as
2. Address what product or service they are asking for.

> Old Way – A company *needs* something and puts out a request. The sales team sees this request, finds out what the prospect is looking for, does its best to show the prospect they can do what they want and at the best value.
>
> New Way – Same as Old Way, but, knows there is a reason the company has this need, and is looking for what has *caused* this need to be funded.

Two Different Value Propositions

There are two value propositions for every deal; one at the executive C-Suite (Cause), and one at the manager level where the product or services is going to be defined and used (Need). Let's call them:

ATL – Above the Line – executive C-Suite
BTL – Below the Line – person/team that will make the purchased item work

Or,

ATL
BTL

So here is the secret that sales people are not trained on, not coached on, and not measured on; there are two value propositions within the buyer's organization, and if the salesperson does not address both value propositions they will be limiting their solution to one value proposition, thereby losing a key competitive advantage.

ATL

The ATL decision is all about the change being required and the return on the investment for this change. What will the ROI be? How will it save them time and money or lower their risks on key challenges and problems they are facing?

It is not the ROI on the product being purchased. It is the ROI of the change being made, where typically, what is being sold is only one contributor to making the change.

For example, take the earlier example of Jim and Susan. Susan has a problem, which is why she needs to make a change to a process or a way her organization is doing something today.

Let's assume the problem that Mark, the CFO, is telling Susan is that the current accounting software will not accommodate an upcoming merger and that IT needs to fix the problem by the start of the new fiscal year.

Susan has assigned Jim to investigate new accounting software solutions, which is how he came up with his decision criteria.

Let's also assume the $200,000 allocated to this project to buy software is only a piece of the solution. New hardware, additional training, 3 more headcount, as well as a new MRP interface module will bring the total expenditure to $1.5M.

A few things to note:

1. The ATL buyers, Susan (VP of IT) and Mark, the CFO, are interested in the ROI of the $1.5M, not just the $200K
2. Mark has stated he can obtain a 30% time savings as well as a 10% faster A/R collection rate with this change, which will also solve the cash flow problem the company is having.
3. Susan also thinks she will be able to save 2% of IT budget, as well as lower the risk of accounting systems that are not auditable, which has been a problem in the past, resulting in 100+ hours of overtime/year. The entire ROI for this project is estimated at $5-10M over two years.
4. The ATL executives could care less what features and functions Jim's (Manager of IT) $200,000 software has. That is Jim's job to handle.

BTL

Jim, the BTL buyer, needs to make sure the CFO and the people in finance get the software they want and it does what they have explained to him they need. John, the Manager of Accounting Operations, is working with Jim to make sure what they buy is easy to use and will do what the accounting team needs. Of note:

1. Nowhere are Jim and John concerned with the MRP interface, the added hardware, the A/R problem, or the 100+ hours of overtime.
2. They have been chartered to get a new software system, and that's what they are doing.
3. Gary, the sales person, is focused on just the software as well, which is why when he did have a chance to meet Susan, and ask her what she wanted in a new software solution, she deferred to Jim.
4. She wanted to talk about her ATL issues, and Gary was doing as he has been trained and coached to do; sell BTL.

When to Create Value - The Split at Stage 2

The buyer has two value propositions for every deal: one ATL and one BTL. A salesperson must recognize this and understand the new paradigm about multiple decision makers and multiple value propositions. By not getting both, the salesperson will capture the BTL value proposition, and leave ATL value on the table.

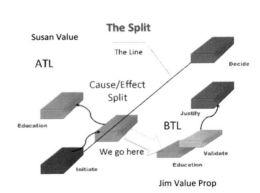

Decision Makers

Finally, there is no such thing as a decision maker anymore; there are two decision makers for every deal and the smart salesperson will capture both early in the sale.

Of course, some deals are so small that the ATL is not engaged at all in the sale. The BTL has the budget authority and what is being purchased has such a small impact on the ATL challenges that ATL really doesn't need or want to get involved.

Be prepared - these deals are getting fewer and fewer. More and more purchases are having too many impacts within companies for the decision to be made by one person.

So when should the sales person go hunting for both value propositions? At Stage 2, Discovery. Stage 1 is when the deal is somewhat qualified for fit and cost, and if it meets a certain qualification metric it advances to Stage 2. Stage 2 is where the buyers are more open to talk about:

- The BTL Value Proposition – What the needs are for the solution they are buying;
- The ATL Value Proposition – Making sure what they are buying will make a dent on at least one or more of their challenges/problems they are trying to fix.

Great sales people are getting to both decision makers early and capturing both value decisions.

It's not about The Dog

A story of a purchase I recently made may make it a bit easier for you to understand the principles of this two-value proposition buyer's dilemma.

A few years back, my wife wanted a dog, and I finally relented and started a search. I was tasked to find the right dog, and after a few weeks of calling around, I found "that perfect" dog. It was at a breeder located in the state of Oregon.

Since we live in San Jose, California, driving up to pick up this dog was not a desirable option. Oregon is at least a 12-hour drive one way, and the thought of a two-day trip to pick up a dog was not on my agenda. There was no way I could take off two days given my work schedule.

The next best option was to put the dog on a flight bound for San Jose. Seems like Delta Airlines offers a pet transfer service from Portland to San Jose. It's about an hour flight and the price was not too bad, so the breeder and I agreed on a final price and a flight. Tomorrow, I would be the proud owner of a new dog... and so would my wife.

After explaining to my wife this glorious news, she proclaimed, "You are not putting that dog on a plane by itself."

Since I clearly did not know why this was not a good idea, she continued. "They put pets in the cargo hold and the oxygen is not as good as it is in the passenger compartment. If that dog is delivered by plane tomorrow, riding in the cargo hold where they put pets, it will arrive having some brain damage due to lack of oxygen."

There would be no more discussion on this topic with her, and me driving 12 hours one way to pick up a dog was still out of the question, so, given my choices, I called the breeder and cancelled the order.

However, during our discussion she asked a question.

"Would you be agreeable to driving half way up here? I'll drive half way down, meet up with you, pass the dog over to you, and then you can drive home with your new pet. Would that be OK?"

Well, a 12 hour round trip to pick up a dog is really not a whole lot better than 24 hours, so I said thanks anyway but we'll have to pass.

About 20 minutes later, she called back again and asked another question. "I just talked to my niece who actually lives in San Jose, and asked her if she would drive half way up here and pick up the dog. She said she would be happy to, and she and I can have lunch as well. So she is willing to drive 6 hours, we'll meet half way, pick up your dog, drive back to San Jose and drop the dog off at your house. All she wants is $100 for gas money.

"Would that work?"

"Done."

We have had Daisy now for about 5 years, and she is a great dog. However, in purchasing the dog, since I was the ATL buyer in this deal,

one thing became perfectly clear for me. For <u>my</u> value proposition:
It had nothing to do with The Dog.

What became clear to me was even in this family purchase; there were two value propositions.

My wife wanted a cuddly dog; a good-sized family-friendly pet she could go on hikes with.

I wanted a dog because I have started traveling more and this change requires some new thinking. I want my family safe when I'm not home and a dog is great protection; the family will not worry or have an "empty house." I want an easy buy process, I don't want to spend a lot of money, and hey, I need to lose a few extra pounds as well.

The Dog – 2 Value propositions

Me - ATL

I travel a lot more
Family safe when I am out of town
Easy to Buy – no hassle
Not a lot of money
Exercise – lose weight

My Wife - BTL

Cuddly
Good Size
Family Friendly
Good Companion
Like to go on dog hikes

Two different value propositions: for my wife, it was all about the dog; for me, my travel schedule has caused a change in my thinking and I want my family safe. The dog was only part of my solution. We bought a new home alarm system, joined a community watch program, and heck, I bought some exercise equipment since I was now committed to losing those few pounds.

It was not about The Dog.

Summary

More and more companies are now training their sales teams on how to capture both value propositions. Business acumen skills, persona skills, and company Line of Business (LoB) skills (what does a CMO, CFO, CEO, etc. actually do) are being taught and coached with greater frequency now.

Contacting ATL and BTL early in the process for their own value proposition requirements are shortening sales cycles, increasing average order sizes and disqualifying deals earlier in the process, which is having a huge jump on pipeline accuracy.

An individual salesperson must take on the requirement of finding out what is causing the change at the ATL level and what the expected return is. The salesperson can determine if what they are selling can contribute to this change—as well as figuring out what the BTL needs. By doing so, they will have more success on every prospect they sell to.

Sales Hack contributed by: Skip Miller, President, M3 Learning

Skip Miller is Founder and President of M3 Learning, a ProActive Sales and Sales Management Training Company based in the heart of Silicon Valley.

As President of M3 Learning, Skip has provided training to hundreds of companies in over 38 countries. He created M3 Learning to "make a

salesperson better on each individual call." M3 Learning's signature selling methodology, ProActive Selling™, is unique in its high-definition focus on the tactics of selling and proactive sales cycle control.

Skip is also the author of the runaway bestseller, ProActive Sales Management. Ranked #1 by Amazon for five consecutive years, it has been translated into multiple languages worldwide and has become the classic textbook for Sales Managers, both new and seasoned alike.

Skip is also the author of four other bestselling books including ProActive Selling, now in its second edition, Knock Your Socks Off Prospecting, Ultimate Sales Tool Kit, ProActive Sales Management and More ProActive Sales Management. His latest book, Selling Above and Below the Line, has just been released to major acclaim.

SALES HACK #11
THE LAST SHALL BE FIRST, THE FIRST SHALL BE LAST

The Hack

Have a senior executive – someone with an operating or technical management role who can really speak for your company – on the FIRST scheduled conversation with a decision-maker-class person from every intrinsically qualified prospective customer.

The Impact

There are 3 big problems that hold back sales velocity at almost every B2B company:

1. It takes too long to find, hire and ramp decent reps.
    a. And even longer to find out they probably aren't going to work out.
    b. And even "ramped" reps still don't know as much as the people who make and deliver the company's products and services.
2. Customers inherently distrust salespeople.
    a. In fact, experience has taught them sales reps will stretch the truth
    b. Because they know sale reps are paid for deals, not customer results.
3. Sales cycles are too long, and deals on the forecast are full of mystery.
    a. Especially with regard to the probability and timing of being signed.

This hack doesn't magically find, hire and ramp reps for you. But it sure makes them useful a lot sooner.

It is one thing to be good enough at sales, but it is a completely different thing to understand a new company, and perhaps a new industry, well enough to serve as a trusted guide for the naturally cautious B2B buyer.

Any competent sales rep should be able to sell an executive briefing with a bona fide expert (thanks Kraig Kleeman for naming this first meeting correctly a very long time ago – maybe this is really Kraig's hack!). In fact, that new hire should be able to sell such a briefing on their very first day on the job. The new hire's lack of company, product and even industry knowledge immediately flips from a liability to an asset.

Of course, it takes honest, humble team players to admit they don't know everything and to put their ego on hold while someone else takes the stage. Oh – wait – "honest, humble team players" – those sound like some pretty good qualities to select for when building a winning sales team.

But what happens in that first substantive meeting? Doesn't the clever sales rep need to control the meeting – and their own executive – in order to make sure the prospect only hears what they should hear, and thinks what they should think? Doesn't someone with real sales chops need to provide some leadership here?

What happens at the first meeting is that the prospect's risk, cost and most importantly **time required to make a decision** drops drastically. The prospect gets the opportunity to confess their true concerns and problems, their worries and horror stories, to someone who has seen it all before and yet is still dedicating their professional life to turning all those problems into opportunities. The prospect no longer has to wonder "what is really going to happen if I take the plunge?" So, more often than not, if both parties agree that it makes sense, they decide to move forward on the spot.

The benefits of putting the Last First are simple:
1. Speed: The prospect usually makes an informed decision NOW because knowledge and trust are brought together at the beginning.
2. Quality: Sales stops working bad "opportunities" in hopes they will become good because they are forced very early to expose the real live prospect to their own senior players – not just a number on a forecast.
3. Customer Knowledge: Everyone learns more by selling than by meeting with each other. Get out of the echo chamber and plunge into the reality of interacting with people who count – prospects and customers about to make a decision!

But We Can't Really Flip the Funnel Like That – Can We?

Objection #1. This can't scale – can it?

After all, our operating and technical executives are very busy in meetings all day long – usually with each other - or desperately being called in for diving catches on deals that are going south.

Fact:

Senior execs at most companies spend most of their time meeting with each other and their staffs, a practice that may "scale", but doesn't produce as much value on any given day as a net new customer. And if the heavy hitters have time to scramble around trying to do diving catches on deals, they have enough time to set deals up that never need to be "saved".

Let's do the math. If you have 5 execs and product experts on staff, each one can easily participate in 4 First Substantive Meetings per day – 30 minutes each. That's 20 "super meetings" every day. My experience is that at least 60% of those meetings will result in a positive outcome–usually an "instant decision" to move forward with confidence. Wait–that's 12 extra high quality deals in flight PER DAY; 3,000 per year. Say the lifetime value of each deal is a mere $20K, we are talking $60M of business for an investment of 2 hours per day by each of 5 execs. That's $12M of accelerated, high quality revenue contribution from each heavy hitter. Looks like it scales to me.

Objection #2. Only salespeople can "sell", right?

Our product, operating, technical executives aren't good salespeople. In fact, they aren't salespeople at all! They'll just screw up the sale by doing something awkward, like prematurely telling the truth.

Fact:

Prospects and customers love the truth, especially from a credible source who knows what she is talking about and must stand behind what she says. Andy Paul calls this "selling with the sharp end of the stick." Sure, you can get lucky and bring down an occasional mammoth by using "sales" tricks and techniques, but real information provided to the prospect NOW simply leaves your competition staring at empty space wondering what happened.

As Dave Kurlan has rigorously established, roughly 3 out of every 4 sales reps already suck, so the reality is that about 75% of your all-important First Substantive Meetings are wasted today. Introducing a truth-telling, problem-solving, credibility-enhancing resource early in the sales process is not likely to make things worse. Even an indifferent sales rep will uncover a gem now and then. This hack turns those lucky hits into wins.

Objection #3: What if a customer cancels the meeting? Or isn't really qualified? Won't the senior exec kill the sales rep or something?

Our execs hate having their time wasted. Sure – they might move a deal or two by setting the table at the First Substantive Meeting, but they also might send the rep to Siberia when the inevitable last minute cancellation happens.

Fact:

It's true–this hack requires a flexible attitude toward an occasional cancellation. But Siberia is really for reps who don't sell much, not for those who schedule so many meetings that an occasional cancellation happens.

Anyway, two things start happening immediately when The Last start showing up for the First Substantive Meeting.

1. Reps get religion in a hurry about getting prospects to both commit to and actually attend scheduled meetings.
2. Prospects don't cancel meetings with big titles as readily as they do with sales reps.
3. When the next step is meeting with a big dog, "qualification" takes on a whole new meaning. Like "qualification", rather than "My happy ears sure would like to believe this is a great opportunity." Why scrub pipelines at the last minute when you can guarantee cleanliness starting with the First Substantive Meeting?

Objection #4: Won't this make my reps weak?

Sales is tough. If product experts and senior execs kill the objections in the first conversations, won't reps just become wimps and sissies, unable to push and pull prospects along the winding path to a closed deal?

Fact:

The immediate purpose of Sales is to add the next great customer to your company's portfolio. Sales reps need lots of capabilities and tools to get the job done, and every opportunity to learn more about the reality of prospect's problems and possible solutions helps that rep get stronger where it counts–in knowing enough to explore more deeply, qualify more precisely and sell more honestly.

To conclude…

Customers are where the action is. And the most important action of all takes place in the very First Substantive Meeting. Done right, this first deep conversation can be used to destroy the worst outcome in sales - "maybe" - and lead to a clear and immediate "yes" or "no", NOW! Bring a senior product, operations or executive leader to that FIRST Substantive Meeting instead of saving them to try to "close" at a LAST meeting and you will get instant sales results. And a better company too.

Sales Hack contributed by: Chris Beall, CEO, ConnectAndSell (Twitter handle: @chris8649)

Chris has been participating in software startups as a founder or at a very

 early stage for most of the past 30 years. Chris's focus has consistently been on creating and taking to market simple products that can be used successfully the first time they are touched, without taking a course or reading a manual. Chris deeply believes that the most powerful part of any software system is the human being that we inappropriately call a "user", and that the value key in software is to let the computer do what it does well (go fast without getting bored) in order to free up human potential. The process of finding these solutions is more one of discovery than invention, and Chris has been lucky enough to have stumbled on, and sold a fair amount of, a few of them.

SALES HACK #12
EMBRACE SILENCE

Sometimes when you think you hear silence, what you really hear is the glorious sound of someone thinking. Try embracing the silence instead of panicking.

Unfortunately most sales people can't. We have the uncontrollable need to fill it in. We repeat ourselves, rephrase what we just said, or to try to fix something that isn't broken. Filling the silence could cost you. You may be missing valuable information, or worse. Sales reps that panic tend to either start dropping the price or answering possible unspoken objections. Sometimes they talk themselves right out a sale they could have had.

If you are talking while they are thinking, you are interrupting them, so before you speak, give them 3 or 4 seconds to figure out what they want to say. If they still don't say anything, it is your job to understand why.

Silence can indicate a few different things:
- Thinking
- Not paying attention
- Trying to make sense of what you just said
- Being angry or irritated

Most of the time, customers are just thinking. Don't interrupt them. If your customer thinks your question is important enough to think about, and is willing to give you information, **embrace the silence**. Give them 3 or 4 seconds to figure out what they want to say. If they still don't say anything, it is your job to understand why. Simply ask something like, "Do you need some clarification?"

With that, they are likely to tell you exactly what you need to know. All you have to do is listen.

Sales Hack contributed by: Liz Heiman, Sales & Marketing Strategist, Alice Heiman, LLC

Leveraging more than 20 years' experience, Liz aligns sales and marketing  initiatives with organizational strategy to help companies achieve revenue goals. Liz leads her clients through strategic planning, brand development and execution of marketing initiatives to enable them to achieve significant growth.

Liz is an accomplished coach, presenter, facilitator and methodologist who partners with her clients to achieve world-class solutions. Liz's consulting includes business assessment, strategic planning, market development, brand development and business improvement processes. Liz creates integrated marketing programs, effectively using social media. Liz is a skilled writer and has written copy for press releases, articles, advertisement, brochures, white papers, blogs and e-blasts.

SALES HACK #13
THE DIVINE WHISPER

Often in our sales campaigns there are consultants and "advisors" that assist our prospects with the evaluation of solutions (ours and our competitors'). When you meet these consultants they tell you that they are just assisting with and organizing the evaluation process so that their client (your prospect) can make the best decision. They participate in most of the meetings you have with the prospect — presentations, demonstrations, reference calls, etc. — but claim they are not part of the decision process.

While it is true that the consultant is not part of the FORMAL decision process, make no mistake, they ARE part of the decision process. There are two important components here.

First, you have to find out if the consultant is favoring you or your competition. About one-half to two-thirds of the way through your sales campaign you need to meet one-on-one with the lead consultant and find out who they are most impressed with. It is very important that you meet with the senior person. If it is one of the big consulting companies, it is the partner or exec VP. If it is a smaller boutique consulting firm, it can be the owner, president or senior executive — whoever closed the deal with the account.

You have to get this person in a room and let them know that you understand that the company is going to make the decision and the consulting firm isn't going to TELL the client what to do. However, you need to say that you understand that when it comes to decision time, the client will ask the consultant something like: "What do you think...who should we go with?" You then ask something like: "When they ask you that and after you state that all the vendors are good, etc., will you be saying you recommend us?"

After you ask this question, listen very carefully. Anything but a "yes" is a "no". If the consultant says something like, "You know, all the vendors are great and we are not going to give any recommendation. We are leaving it up to the client to make the decision.", that is a clear "NO". Sorry, but you are losing and the consultant is going to recommend your competition.

Remember, anything but a YES is a NO. All the BS the consultant will tell you is basically a long way of saying, "We are not recommending you."

The second thing is if the consultant says "Yes", you are the winner. What you have done is ask them to give the client the "Divine Whisper". The Divine Whisper is when the client asks the consultant what they think about all the vendors and the consultant says something like: "You know, all the vendors are good .... blah blah blah .... However, ABC Co. (you) is really impressive. They do so many things differently. I'm leaning toward them." THAT is the Divine Whisper.

The consultant doesn't tell the client the decision; they whisper in their ear the way they suggest they should go. And guess what? 90% of the time the client goes in the direction of the Divine Whisper. I hope you get many Divine Whispers.

Sales Hack contributed by: Stephen D'Angelo, Vice President Global Sales, Hearsay Social

Stephen D'Angelo is a software industry veteran of over 25 years building high performance global sales organizations and running venture backed technology companies. He currently is the VP of Global Sales for Hearsay Social, a Silicon Valley company. His leadership roles have been in some of

the most innovative market segments including social, mobile and big data. Prior to joining Hearsay Social, Steve was Senior VP of Sales for Kony Solutions, the leader in mobile application development solutions. Other market leading companies Steve has held leadership positions with include Jive Software, IMI, and Optum Software. Steve was also co-founder and CEO of Spring Lake Technologies which provided innovative predictive software that enabled companies to hire and develop high performing sales professionals. Steve has spoken to audiences worldwide on the topic of using world-class methods to build and scale high performance, highly motivated sales organizations. Steve sits on the advisory board of early stage companies in addition to Montclair University Business School and a school for children with autism.

60

SALES HACK #14
LINKEDIN MESSAGING SECRETS

Social selling involves many aspects and messaging is a centerpiece. If you're in B2B sales, then that means LinkedIn. Sales reps, managers and marketing come together to bring LinkedIn into the fold of corporate marketing efforts. Since users must send from their profiles, there are many interlocking elements including training, tools and a new look at social media policies.

Messaging campaigns brings together human interaction, processes and management tools as LinkedIn cannot be automated like many of the other social media platforms.

Still there are some nifty shortcuts to running a campaign and they can really free you up. They can also be used by a Virtual Assistant (VA) to speed them up as they work on your behalf. We've mastered the finest details and I can share some of the best parts here.

Lead generation includes extending and accepting invitations. It includes reaching out to people already in your network as well. Some of it is reactive, but the most insightful professionals will take things into their own hands and implement outbound campaigns.

A Shortcut to Sending Messages

People have been adopting standardized messages for use in LinkedIn like they have everywhere else. People customize them a bit and send them on.

This is the way lots of forward thinking people do it:
1. Keep the standard text in a Word file
2. Select the right text
3. Copy it (CTRL-V)
4. Go to the right place and paste it in
5. Maybe customize it a little
6. Send it off

It's a little tedious, but luckily, there are solutions that help a lot. I use a great free tool called Auto Text Expander (AutoTextExpander.com) and it plugs right into my Chrome browser.

With Auto Text Expander, I simply type ";**TL1**" wherever I want message #1 to appear and ";**TL4**" wherever I want message #4.

I use a lot of customized messages, but I started from 4 or 5 that I "cloned off." I keep a little cheat sheet.

This might be a place to start"

- Invite to someone you recently talked to (;iR1)
- Invite to someone who will probably recall who you are (;iP1)
- Invite to a total stranger that you want to connect to (;iT1)
- A thank you message for when someone invites you on LinkedIn (;aA1)
- A thank you message for when someone accepts your LinkedIn invite (;aS1)

I simply accept, hit reply, type ";**iR1**", customize it a bit from something I know or discover in their profile or on a call and send it off.

Taking it a bit further we add tags to these people so we can keep extra tabs on them.

Messaging campaigns

The very tools that you use to manage your inviting and responding can be the centerpiece of your outbound LinkedIn messaging campaigns for lead generation. This is the mix:

1. Highly targeted LinkedIn advanced searches
2. Carefully crafted messages, sometimes with content
3. 1 by 1 manual delivery of each campaign message (with Auto Text Expander)
4. 1 by 1 tagging for individuals messaged (CRM type tracking)
5. Repeated manual, automated drip campaign process

Even though they are highly targeted, campaigns can deliver lots of results if you have decent sized network — way more than you are allowed to see. The results must be divided up into smaller pieces, like slices of bread. There are two very good methods of doing this.

Industry is a mutually exclusive selection. For example, if you sell to the technology industry you might target computer hardware, computer software, information technology, computer networking and security, telecommunications and others. Divide up the campaign one industry at a time.

Another terrific way to filter search results is by Company Size. This brings in people whose "current employer" says they have this many people on their company page. That's a mouthful. This feature is only available to premium subscribers.

TOGETHER, these two filters let you slice and dice up your searches that may also include some keywords/keyphrases or even a job title.

It's all managed with LinkedIn tags and lots of attention to detail, returning throughout the day to update tagging data.

Many people choose to have an assistant or even a virtual assistant do this tedious campaign messaging work.

Links in Messages

There are some pretty important things to think about when including links in the messages you send on LinkedIn and they greatly affect your success in messaging, especially in campaigns.

Links can be deceiving, dangerous and an obstacle to your message getting through. Fortunately, things are a little better in LinkedIn than they are in other areas like email.

Here is one of our best practices for using links in messages, particularly in LinkedIn messages. Limit what people see when dealing with long, ugly URL's. For example:

www.BigCloudCompanyInc.com/techspecs/final/2015/12/03/Big-Cloud-Product-Comparison-For-Small-Business.PDF

Spring for some domains and use them to simplify what people see. Clicks will go up. Behind the scenes you simply buy a domain and forward to the ugly one using a simple "301 Redirect". That ugly link above then looks like:

www.CompareBCCOptions.com

Custom LinkedIn Invitations on Mobile

While this is not a way to run a campaign, it is a good way to get more out of the LinkedIn invites you send using your mobile phone. Most people press the big blue CONNECT button when they are looking at someone's profile. It sends off a generic invite and that's that. We all know we're supposed to send a custom invite unless maybe you are expecting it right then.

Well, if you look in the right places you can solve this mobile messaging problem quite simply. You CAN send a custom invitation from an iPhone, just not with the CONNECT button. It seems kind of odd, but that's the way it is. This is what to do:

1. Get to their profile on phone, where you see the CONNECT button
2. Look in the upper right corner for the *** and click on it
3. You should see options to "Customize Invite" or "Forward Profile"
4. Pick Customize Invite, type in your message and send

I'm looking for an Auto Text Expander mobile app down the road. In the meantime, there are some others like Type Snippets to try.

Sales Hack contributed by: Mike O'Neil, Co-Founder, Integrated Alliances & LinkedIn Rockstar

Mike inspires and educates his audiences with Vision, Energy and Style

borrowing from classic rock music to harness relationship building for Social Selling and Online Marketing. Mike serves as the LinkedIn Practice Manager for Sales Lead Automation, a division of the Integrated Marketing Summit and he coaches numerous executives and celebrities from the music industry. Find Mike at http://MikeIsOnline.com.

SALES HACK #15
A SOCIAL SELLING GUIDE FOR BABY BOOMERS

Sales experts talk about Social Selling as a brand new skill. The activities actually seem new because they are so old. Today's fresh breed of salespeople - and some sales managers - have never sold before the advent of Marketing Automation, CRM systems, or the Internet, so they never knew another way.

Here is a break down of the three core activities of Social Selling with some historical perspectives and suggested actions to update your skills.

Social Networking:

Sales is a people business; it's about relationships. New sales reps are taught the principle of 'Know, Like, Trust' in Sales 101 class. Whether you followed Dale Carnegie's *How to Win Friends and Influence People* (1936), or Harvey Mackay's questionnaire entitled *66 Things You Should Know About Your Customer,* the underlying principle is the same; the shopkeeper's ledger gave way to the businessman's Rolodex which gave way to the salesperson's software like ACT!, Goldmine, or Salesforce.com. LinkedIn and Twitter are just the latest iterations of these tools. A benefit of social networks is that customers update their own information; therefore it is current, and offers insights into that person's interests, objectives, and priorities. Who doesn't want to read their prospect's mind?

Clients often ask whether senior salespeople can adapt. They can and they should! Senior staff they have built their networks through years of engagement in business relationships, industry associations, community involvement and personal interests.

As an example, one of my "students" is an executive with one of the largest privately held insurance firms in the nation. After his company's LinkedIn training program, he was one of the most active users among their entire company. He recognized the networking power of LinkedIn. In 2016, he will celebrate his 50-year anniversary with the company!

Here are three ways to improve your Social Networking skills with LinkedIn:
1. Invite people from your contact system every day. A custom

invitation is best; replace the default message with something like *"I'm finally getting serious about LinkedIn and I wanted us to be connected."*

2. Make a habit of inviting people that you meet in your daily business life: prospects, suppliers, co-workers, association members, alumni, etc.

3. Check *'People You May Know'* for connection suggestions from LinkedIn, based on commonalities of industry, location, groups, and other factors you share.

Social Prospecting:

As a new salesperson, I eagerly anticipated the delivery of the weekly business journal to scan it for events. Are there any relevant promotions or job changes in the 'Movers and Shakers' section? What about a new company moving to town or a recent merger? These trigger events were prospecting gold because it gave me something relevant upon which to base an initial outreach call. Later, when I was a sales manager for a business software company, I would do drive-alongs with my salespeople in remote cities. Since any company with computers was a prospect, I would scan the company names on skyscrapers and ask, "Are they a customer? What about them? Are they a customer?"

Today, the world moves too fast to wait one week for "ink on trees" or to drive around looking for smokestacks. Using social networks for prospecting is much more efficient. There are two separate activities; *Social Listening*, which is similar to the business journal practice and *Social Searching*, both of which involve searching for criteria like a job title, company name, an industry, location or company size.

Here are three ways to improve your Social Prospecting skills with LinkedIn:

1. Set up a *Saved Search* in LinkedIn so you get fresh leads emailed to you every week. It's like Google Alerts, except the results are LinkedIn members who fit your ideal customer profile.

2. Use LinkedIn's *Keep in Touch* feature (browser) or *Connected* app (for iPhone or Android) to catch trigger events about your connections: promotions, work anniversaries, job changes, news mentions, or birthdays.

3. Follow *Individuals* and *Target Companies* on LinkedIn and Twitter so posts and news shows up in your Home Page feed or Twitter stream.

Social Content Sharing:

When I started in field sales, my company's marketing department shipped me boxes of brochures, data sheets, catalogs, and even a few wall posters. I kept them all in the trunk of my black 1986 Ford Taurus. A big part of my job then was being a content distributor. I drove around Atlanta meeting with customers and prospects and decided which content to share with them to build relationships and advance a sale. Often, I would hand-write something in the border to customize the content— "Here's a case study of a customer with a similar challenge." Occasionally I'd read something in a trade magazine and run off copies at Kinkos to share with my customers. In those days, my trunk was my content library and my car was the distribution medium. Fast forward 30 years and smart salespeople are doing the same thing with social networks. Digital content is readily available from marketing and industry websites. It's simple to share it via social networks. The best salespeople will still add their personal comments to customize it for their audience. This raises their value in the customer's eyes and influences the purchasing decision.

Here are three ways to improve your Social Content Sharing:

1. Comment on LinkedIn posts or Tweets in your area of expertise. Pay attention to who else responds.
2. Share content that your network would find valuable. Find it on your company website, blog, or LinkedIn/Twitter page or industry news sites.
3. Create original content of your own and publish it using LinkedIn's long-form publishing feature or setup your own blog.

Newspapers, the Rolodex, and Kinkos have all faded from use, but building relationships and sharing valuable content never goes out of style. Learn how to combine your mastery of sales fundamentals with a competent use of new social selling tools and you will be selling like it's 1999!

Sales Hack contributed by: Kurt Shaver, CEO, The Sales Foundry

Kurt Shaver is a leading Social Selling speaker and trainer for corporate  sales teams. His experience as a Silicon Valley sales executive and, later, a Salesforce.com consultant, taught him how to implement new technologies and skills across sales organizations. He is the creator of the Social Selling Boot Camp and has spoken at events like Dreamforce, Sales 2.0, Sales Velocity Summit, and LinkedIn's Sales Connect conference. Kurt writes a top-ranked social selling blog and is a regular contributor to Selling Power, Top Sales World, and Business2Community. Clients include Hewlett Packard, TelePacific Communications, Nexus/Dimension Data, Maritz, and City National Bank.

SALES HACK #16
FOCUS TO EXCEED YOUR NUMBER

A little hint on how to improve your win rate–focus! By putting a few guidelines in place, sales reps could spend more of their time on the right deals, meet their quota and sell a few deals extra while they're at it.

I heard an interesting statistic from my good friends at the reputable firm CSO Insights. Their research states that sales reps lose 54% of the deals that are in their forecast. So that means sales reps are spending 54% of their time on the wrong deals – what a waste!

That statistic resonated so well with me personally. For the past 8 years, I had to face a board of directors and present our company's performance to our quarterly number. Most of the time we met our top line number, but it was always a struggle at the end of the quarter to pull in deals–we never had a handle on deals that would support the forecast early on.

So here's 3 tenets to help with focusing on the right deals to increase win rates:

1.   **Focus on the ideal customer profile**: Make sure you are focusing on the right leads and opportunities. They should be the right size–know the revenue or number of employees that your company has had the best success with. Make sure the role that will sponsor your deal has the right authority to get things done. The role that sponsors your product will own the problem and therefore have the urgency to do something. Make sure they have the confidence and ability to pull in the right people that would make up the buying team and that they can help you convince them of your value proposition and how they will benefit and make a return. Market or industry is another attribute of ideal customer profile. Understand and promote the value proposition for certain markets by reviewing your solution's adoption and benefits within the top markets represented by your existing customer base. Some markets, especially within tech, will typically be early adopters of new technology.

2.   **Apply a rigorous sales process:** Identify and apply the right stages to your sales process. These stages should be made up of your most successful active customers and the process that the sales rep followed to close the deal. Examples of stages could be related to actions are "Qualifying, Defining, Demo, Contracts Pending" or "Current State, Solution

Alignment, Proofpoint, Pricing Alignment" — a definition of each opportunity's current state and status. Clear exit criteria such as milestones or activities that occur while the opportunity is within that stage have to be defined. This is important for an opportunity to advance from one stage to the next. This helps the sales rep to understand and focus on the next steps to advance the opportunity to the next stage and ultimately convert it in the optimum time. Thinking about your process in three parts — "The Beginning", "The Middle" and "The End" — is a great way to understand what stages and milestone are important to your company. Identify the activity from The Beginning where you state the reason they want your product, to The Middle where you are doing enough discovery to find the real pain points, and The End where you have aligned your solution with everyone involved to move forward with the deal. By the very end, you should be able to tie back what they say at The End to your original and high-level valuation proposition you promised at The Beginning. A couple of things to look out for — make sure you are focusing on the right opportunities by only promoting leads to opportunities that meet the ideal customer profile and that have the appropriate urgency and access to budget in addition to authority and need. Also, apply different sales processes so you can have appropriate metrics to the right cohort. For example, don't have a blended view of everything — separate out Enterprise Sales from SMB Sales and Hunters from Farmers.

3. Watch momentum: Velocity of opportunities is a great place to focus. If a good opportunity gets stuck, you must examine why. Did you do enough discovery? Are you calling high enough? Also look for problems in opportunities, especially as they advance in each stage. Examples of problems could be that an opportunity is going too long without the next meeting scheduled, or you have advanced a deal far enough to send a proposal but have not heard back in a reasonable amount of time. It's important to stay in contact with the sponsor and know they see the value of the next step in the process. A deal that goes too long - usually a week or two without a valuable milestone being met - could end up falling out of the pipeline.

As you focus on these three tenets to find the right leads and opportunities to work, always be looking ahead to make sure you have enough to fill any gap you may have to meet the number for the current sales period. It is important to roll into the following quarter with the right amount in your pipeline to meet that number. Metrics to watch would be lead touches (ex. emails sent, calls or meetings), deal touches (ex. meetings, demos, check-ins) and number of deals in the pipeline.

For B2B sales, our research shows that this will help sales teams win at least 25% more deals. Trying to cover every opportunity diminishes the chances of meeting the number. This is not that complex – it is simply a matter of understanding where to focus and what the next steps are will drive more deals.

Sales Hack contributed by: Jim Eberlin, CEO, TopOpps

Experienced entrepreneur and founder of two market leading companies in Host Analytics and Gainsight, Jim is currently the Founder and CEO of

TopOPPS, a sales pipeline predictability solution that uses intelligent mobile prompting and big data analytics to bring clarity and efficiency to the sales pipeline. As a result, sales executives can forecast better and move deals through the pipeline quicker. Sales representatives can spend more time selling and less time on data entry.

SALES HACK #17
WOMEN IN SALES

I was an anomaly to be raised in a family-run sales business headed by a strong woman yet I never saw any more women leaders for many years in my sales career – and few successful female peers in the sales role.

I went into technology sales many years ago intentionally — to have what I thought would be a rewarding career AND for the opportunity to make the same compensation as my male peers through sales commissions. That's right – I chose that path on purpose and loved the idea of being paid for hitting my sales numbers.

Why sales? You might say it was in my blood. Before I was a teenager I ran a successful lemonade stand and owned a popular seasonal business making holiday ornaments. Those endeavors didn't seem odd because I grew up in a family-run fine apparel business where my CEO Grandmother was my business role model, and she taught me how to sell both consultatively and through referrals at a very young age.

In the tech world, which I entered in my early 20's, scotch and cigars were often awarded – and my title was "Salesman" – but that didn't bother me. As a single parent providing for my family, management could call me most anything as long as I was in the top 10% on the old, handwritten leaderboard. I was happy.

Flash forward to today, and I'm about present and participate in the largest software conference in the world – where women will be featured more prominently than ever. Every day there will be discussions about diversifying technology roles in general, the low percentage of women in leadership positions, and how we can work together to see more successful women in sales and sales leadership roles.

That's why I think this is the "Year of Women in Sales." For the first time, many conversations are going on about diversity and unconscious bias. One conference I attended early this year, Accelerate 2015, had a panel discussion on how women and men are different in business. I've not seen that happen on a main stage in years – maybe ever. It is often, when discussed, a breakout room session, with little thought to the goals or results.

More than ten years ago, best-selling sales author and keynote speaker Jill Konrath shared her frustration for the lack of women on the main stage as speakers about B2B sales topics, and soon after created a group for like-minded women sales experts to share ideas and collaborate. Jill handed the reins over to me a couple of years ago, and in 2015 we re-branded it to Women Sales Pros. What began as a community for like-minded sales experts (who happen to be women) is now a well-received and referred to community for anyone who wants to learn more about sales and sales leadership. Its side benefit is that it is inspiring young women new to sales and tenured women in sales looking for direction to become successful sales leaders.

No One Wants to be the Poster Girl Leading this Cause

When I was asked to write about women in sales, I hesitated. After all, I am a teacher of B2B sales strategy, with onboarding, prospecting, and sales leadership as my specialties. I work with a predominantly male-focused population and don't want to be pigeon-holed as a "women's champion". Most of my female colleagues feel similarly.

At the same time, I have seen such little movement of women into higher sales leadership roles in the companies I work with, and a lack of diversity in the make-up of sales teams. It is natural for me to speak about what I know for sure, and that is what I'm sharing here.

Great News for Young Women Looking Into a Sales Career

Most college students are influenced by their parents when choosing their vocation and major. I am happy to report that there are over 20 universities around the U.S. who now offer a Sales Major program and, according to the Sales Education Foundation, over 80 universities offer some sort of a sales minor or certificate program. Take a look at their 2014 list of schools. In the Boston area alone, Bentley launched a Professional Sales Degree last year, and Boston College is launching a minor in sales as well.

What does this have to do with women in sales? Many young women choose a career in marketing over sales because marketing degrees are widely offered and sales has had a bad rap. Most parents do not suggest to their daughters to consider a career in sales due to those few negative selling stereotypes we all know. Now with sales degrees on the rise, and amazing women leaders gaining visibility, this is changing.

Great News for Women Starting Out in B2B Sales Positions

There has NEVER been a better time for aspiring sellers to find top content online to learn better ways to do their job well. Unlike the days of old, where we had to buy a limited choice of author's books or learn from a limited amount of local mentors, today you can build a career based on the tremendous insight online. The biggest issue now is simply what to read and what not to read – who to listen to and who to pass up.

Any young person – male or female – can watch hours of webinars and listen to hundreds of archived audios and podcasts for professional development. Combine that with great insight about role specialization, such as the SDR (Sales Development Rep) role, and it is simple to craft your own plan for growth and development with easily accessed content. Companies like Pipeliner Sales, ConnectAndSell, Guidespark, InsideSales.com and many others are making an effort to search out diverse candidates instead of the old tech hiring habit of referring more of your buddies, who are much like you.

Great News for Tenured Women Sellers

More mentors and role models area available for you than ever before! We are finally seeing conferences and events with top women sales leaders and women sales experts on the main stage. Companies like Salesforce.com are consciously seeking diversity and are reflecting that throughout their events. The first *Women in Sales Awards, North America* event was held in 2015 in Boston, and is slated to be held in 2016 in Chicago. I was honored to be a judge for the event and was extremely impressed with the accomplishments of the women sellers and sales leaders nominated.

Just a few years ago the only women on the main stage at a B2B sales conference were often marketers, not sales leaders or sales experts – or they were communication or presentation experts. Now we see great women leaders, like Emmanuelle Skala, VP Sales at Influitive; Liz Cain, Senior Director of Worldwide Business Development at Netsuite; and Sandy Carter, GM at IBM – and many more amazing women are part of this group. It's important because when you are a keynote speaker you gain visibility, opportunity, and a tremendous chance to impact more attendees.

More Work to be Done

Last year, Alex Hisaka of LinkedIn published an infographic called Trends of Women in Sales which showed that the percentage of women in sales has increased just 3% in the last ten years. The <u>Bridge Group</u> published a widely viewed post, <u>Hiring More Women in Technology</u> that is exceptional in explaining ways companies can be more successful in hiring more women sellers. Three things mentioned are to consider the perks your company offers, have visible successful women involved in some way in the interview process, and check your common use of "war words" like "quota killer" or "sales assassin". One large sales force I know with a 90% male - 10% female sales rep ratio does two of these three things plus they are not conscious of the very masculine environment around them.

The Payoff for Women is Great

Companies who broaden their pool of sales candidates to consider more top women for roles gain ROI because they have widened the net for more "A" players and winning candidates. Many companies are still looking at only 50% of the workforce seriously. I hope that is something we don't see much longer as younger leaders change things up in hiring. For women considering sales or who are in sales and unsure of their path, the payoff of a long career in selling is unlimited.

The profession of sales to me is like craftspersonship. It is part science, and part art. Like a wood carver or cabinet maker, sellers gain invaluable nuances over time to become masters at their craft. There are some great women in the world who could be fantastic sellers, and a career in professional selling has limitless possibilities. Many sales roles have no cap on commissions and we all know case after case of top sales reps making more money than their company's C-level executives. There is also great flexibility in most sales roles, which as a single parent helped me to be present for my family while also hitting my numbers.

The other great thing about professional selling is that you always know where you stand. Your sales numbers speak for you – if they are down, you know what you need to do. It could not be simpler than finding products or services that you are passionate about, and sharing your fascination, curiosity, passion and insights with potential buyers.

I look forward to the time when this is not a topic of interest because we all figured it out, and no one is blaming the other for the issues – it's solved.

Sales Hack contributed by: Lori Richardson, CEO, Score More Sales & President, Women Sales Pros

Lori and Score More Sales (www.scoremoresales.com) work with mid-sized tech and distribution companies, helping the frontline reps and

 managers with a sure-fire prospecting approach. A former Franklin Covey facilitator, Lori also challenges receptive CEOs to new approaches for revenue increases. These approaches might include a change in recruiting strategy, putting a better sales system in place, or improving sales leadership to accelerate sales and grow the bottom line.

With an award-winning blog and a book series called "50 Days to Build Your Sales", Lori will release "Sales GEMs- How to Attract Buyers, Shine, and Score More Sales" Q1 2016. Lori also speaks to women in sales roles and to CEOs on creative ways to grow the percentage of women in sales and leadership positions as President of Women Sales Pros (www.womensalespros.com)

Find her on twitter @scoremorsales and elsewhere on social platforms, or at lori@scoremoresales.com.

SALES HACK #18
MAKE CLOSING EASY BY ASKING TOUGH QUESTIONS

Closing the deal doesn't have to be hard

Salespeople can make closing hard by failing to ask the tough questions. The way to be sure the sale is moving forward is to ask questions, listen and respond appropriately. This helps the buyer on their journey rather than forcing the close.

There are specific questions you should ask. To make sure you do, it's best to prepare by developing a plan for each sales call.

I know if you ask these questions you will have most of the information you need to collaborate with buyers and help them on their journey.

10 Questions to Ask

1. How will our solution meet your needs?
2. What other solutions have you considered?
3. Who will be involved in making the decision?
4. What is the best way to include everyone involved in the decision making process?
5. What is your budget?
6. On what factors will you make your decision?
7. What is your timeline for implementation?
8. What is your timeline for making a decision?
9. Is there anything else we need to discuss?
10. What are our next steps?

Getting the answers to these questions assures you know where the deal is going. The answers keep you focused on the customer and how they will buy.

You may be thinking, this is easier said than done. It's easy if you plan and practice. You have to work these questions into the conversation so that they seem natural and not abrupt. In order to get honest answers to any of these questions you need to be talking to someone who trusts you. That means before you can ask tough questions, you have to build the relationship. If you have a relationship with the people involved in making the decisions and they trust you, you can easily ask these questions and get the needed answers. **What will Sales Hack do?**

Sales Hack will use these questions to prepare for every sales call. He will figure out which of these questions to ask at each point in the sales process. Before asking for the business he will make sure he has the answers.

When he reviews a deal with his manager he will use these questions to show the progress he has made in moving the sale forward and will discuss what remains to be done by which questions have not been answered. Planning each sales call and determining which questions to ask at each step in the sales process will make it easy for Sales Hack to close more deals.

Sales Hack contributed by: Alice Heiman, Founder & Chief Sales Officer, Alice Heiman, LLC

Alice Heiman, creator of the Sales Success System and sales thought leader

was named Best Sales Blogger Innovator 2013 and one of the Top 100 Most Innovative Sales Bloggers 2015. She is a regular contributor to HubSpot, Nimble, RingLead and Selling Power blogs. Alice's specialties lie in networking, social selling, and effective sales strategies for innovative companies. Alice is an extraordinary sales coach and networker whose clients consistently increase sales 30% or more.

SALES HACK #19
TIME IS THE ULTIMATE SALES HACK

Part 1 - The True Measure of Sales Productivity

Time is the ultimate sales hack.

To hack something is to unlock the potential and possibilities within it. If you want to hack sales, then you have to unlock the potential of time to measurably improve your sales productivity.

As Chris Beall, CEO of ConnectAndSell, wrote in his foreword to a new edition of my book, **Zero-Time Selling, 10 Essential Steps To Accelerate Every Company's Sales**, "Time is the field upon which sales is played."

The hard truth of that statement can't be avoided. You can push and pull on every imaginable lever, and employ every possible "sales hack," to control the multiple variables that have an impact on sales productivity. But unless these hacks provide an improvement on the basic equation of sales productivity, it's doubtful whether they'll lend more than a marginal improvement in sales performance.

Unfortunately, we've become too casual with our use of the term sales productivity. It's interchangeably used with sales performance, when, in fact, the two are very different. (As I show below, a sales rep can improve their performance without necessarily becoming more productive.)

It's important that sales leaders start examining productivity in sales in the same manner that productivity is viewed in other professions.

In economic terms, productivity is a measure of the rate of output for a given unit of input. How many items can be manufactured in an hour? For instance, economists measure the economic productivity of the American worker as the amount of good and services produced per hour of labor.

Therefore, true sales productivity should be expressed as the rate of output, as measured in revenue dollars sold, for a given unit of input, which is an hour of selling time.

A time-based productivity measure is a new concept for most sales leaders.

If you're like most managers, you measure the length of your sales cycle in days, weeks or months. The problem with that approach is that days, weeks and months are merely a measure of how long your prospects take to make a decision. These aren't a measure of how much selling time you've invested to win the order.

You should be measuring your sales cycle in selling hours. How many selling hours do your sales reps need to invest in order to move a prospect from initial interest to a decision? That is a true measure of sales productivity.

Sales reps have a fixed inventory of time to use for all the tasks associated with their job. Some portion of that time will be spent on non-revenue producing activities, like paperwork and meetings. The balance of hours should be selling time during which sales reps exclusively engage with prospects. Assuming that they are adequately trained and capable, the quantity of selling time a sales rep invests in a sales opportunity is the variable that ultimately dictates their sales productivity.

Improving sales productivity doesn't mean that you are solely focused on strategies to increase the number of hours of selling time a sales rep has. You should be doing that as a matter of course by working to eliminate the obstacles and overhead that reduce your sales reps available inventory of selling time. This will give your reps more time to sell. But, this won't impact their productivity (though it should improve their performance).

Here's the rough math of sales productivity. Assume that there are 2080 work hours in a year and that 50% of these work hours are actual selling time. If Sales Rep (we'll call her Alysa) closes orders that result in $2,000,000 of revenue in a fiscal year then her sales productivity is equal to $1,923 per hour of selling time.

If you give Alysa 5% more selling hours, and she sells with her same level of productivity, then she can increase her sales performance to $2,100,000 in a fiscal year. If you give Alysa 5% more selling hours, AND help her increase her sale productivity by 5%, then she could increase her performance by more than 10%.

While you may find it difficult to permanently eliminate the bureaucratic hurdles than rob sales reps of selling time, changes in sales productivity that are due to amplifying the skills, expertise and capabilities of a sales rep are more durable and impactful.

As a sales leader, you should focus your efforts and your investment in the hiring practices, professional development and technology that will enable your sales reps to generate more revenue per hour of selling time.

Your objective should be to maximize the value a sales rep can deliver during each sales interaction with a prospect in order to reduce the number of such sales interactions required to move the prospect across the finish line to a winning decision. That's how you increase sales productivity.

Part 2 - The Race to Zero - Hacking Sales Time

You can talk about any other tip or technique for hacking sales that you want. They might help at some level of performance. But if you aren't hacking your sales time then to some degree you're wasting your time.

The goal of a sales leader should be to continually reduce the amount of time required to complete every customer facing sales process.

In theory, if a process is continually refined and improved, the time required to execute it will begin to approach zero. That is what the Race to Zero means. Zero is the point at which sales productivity will be optimally optimized.

- Zero is the percentage of inbound sales leads that are never followed up.
- Zero is the amount of time required to follow up on inbound sales leads.
- Zero is the amount of time required to respond to customer sales and support questions.
- Zero is the amount of time each hour that SDRs are not having sales conversations.
- Zero is the amount of time each hour that Account Execs are not talking to qualified sales opportunities.

How do you hack your sales time to accelerate your own Race to Zero?

1. Put your customer first

Selling is about the customer. It's not about you or the various steps of your sales process. In an interview with the Harvard Business Review in 2013, Jeff Bezos, founder and CEO of Amazon, succinctly defined selling when he said "We don't make money when we sell things. We make money when we help the customer make a purchase decision." That's selling in a nutshell. We don't win until our customer wins.

Given that research shows that your prospects increasingly want to make decisions faster, you'll hack time out your sales process if you focus your account planning on those steps you can take that will compress the prospect's decision making process. At any point in your sales process you must be able to answer this question: What information does the prospect need from me right now that will enable them to move at least one step closer to making a decision?

2. Define sales as a service
First and foremost, sales is a service that you provide to your customer. It is not something you do to a customer. It's an iterative, collaborative process to help the customer make a decision that will enable them to achieve a particular business objective(s).

If the customer perceives an authentic desire on your part to serve then that becomes a critical and essential element of building trust with the buyer. And if trust accelerates the speed of economic relationships, as Stephen M.H. Covey demonstrated in his best-selling book The Speed of Trust, then having "serving the prospect" as the focal point of your sales activities will facilitate and accelerate their buying process. And, increase your sales productivity.

A service-oriented seller knows before every sales touch exactly what value they are going to deliver to the prospect that will enable them to move at least one step forward in their buying process.

3. Commit to absolute responsiveness
Being first to respond is not the same as being responsive. In fact, in sales the race doesn't go the swift. It goes to the responsive.

Responsiveness in sales has a very specific definition. Responsiveness = Value + Speed. Value is information in any form (questions, insights, data, wisdom, context) that helps the customer move at least one step closer to making a decision. Value delivered with speed is responsiveness.

Being responsive is perhaps the easiest and fastest way to increase sales productivity. It creates meaningful sales differentiation with a buyer.

And, most importantly of all, the ability to be responsive is completely under the control of you as a sales leader or individual sales rep. There's no training required. Your ability to be responsive is not dependent on anyone else. It's as simple as just doing it.

Responsiveness starts at the top. It is a central element of the buyer's experience with you as a seller. It is a statement that you respect their time and that you are committed to helping them earn a strong ROI on the time that they've invested in you.

4. Accelerate your sales processes

Too many sellers get hung up on their own sales processes. The steps in the process become rigid, static obstacles to helping your prospects make fast and favorable decisions. Sales processes are all about you and not about the customer.

- Document your sales processes. It's true that you can't accelerate a process that doesn't exist. Most sales organizations do not have documented sales processes. In surveys I have conducted of nearly 300 sales organizations, nearly 72% responded that they didn't have defined, written sales processes. In other words, they're making it up as they go along. How can you set expectations for responsiveness, serving the customer with maximum sales productivity, if you don't have defined processes that sellers should follow?

- Define metrics for key customer facing sales activities. These same sales organizations that did not have documented sales processes also did not have metrics for their key sales processes. How long should it take to follow up a lead? How long should it take to respond to a customer voice mail or email? Obviously, you can't engage in a Race to Zero if you don't know where the starting line is and therefore can't determine whether you're going fast or slow.

- Your sales processes have to be measured, examined, refined and improved on an ongoing basis. This is how you begin to approach Zero. Define metrics for each of your key customer facing sales processes. Collect your data and review it weekly in sales meetings Then, at least once per quarter, make a change to at least one process that will accelerate it. Redefine your new metrics based on your change and start the process over.

5. Hire and train the right people

In my book, Zero-Time Selling, I discussed the need to sell with the Sharp End of the Stick. By this I meant, selling with people who have the knowledge and expertise to help their customers make faster, favorable decisions.

To reach Zero-Time, your objective should be to increase the productivity of a sales rep by helping them maximize the value that they can deliver during each sales interaction with a prospect. Maximizing the impact of every sales interaction with a prospect will reduce the number of sales interactions required to help the prospect cross the finish line to a winning decision.

In inside sales organizations, where the model is to hire inexperienced salespeople as SDRs, you'll always achieve increased productivity with more knowledge and expertise in those positions. The key becomes to hire people with greater skills upfront or to retain the SDRs who have attained great proficiency at their work (instead of promoting them just as they start measurably increasing their productivity). This also includes creating a sales environment that engenders a high degree of job satisfaction in what is a demanding and relentless job environment.

6. Invest in tools and technology to support your process
Increasingly there are tools being introduced to the market that can support your Race to Zero. These extend well beyond the CRM system that has become table stakes for any sales organization. In particular, research and invest in those tools that can measurably move the needle on the productivity of your individual SDRs and AEs.

Consider starting with one of the simple email tracking apps. These can be wonderful sources of real-time customer intelligence that can be immediately actionable by a sales rep. Instead of waiting and wondering whether a prospect has opened and read your email, now you know, and be responsive, the instant it happens.

For more information on tools to help improve your sales productivity check out the blogs of Miles Austin at www.fillthefunnel.com and Nancy Nardin at www.smartsellingtools.com. They are experts on existing and emerging sales tools that can help you win your Race to Zero.

Also, check out the system of our lead sponsor, ConnectAndSell. If your business fits their ideal customer profile then you'll rocket ahead in the Race to Zero with their system.

Sales Hack contributed by: Andy Paul, Author, Zero Time Selling and Amp Up Your Sales

Andy Paul is a leading sales acceleration expert, author, speaker and coach. He is the author of two books: the Amazon best-seller **Amp Up Your**  **Sales: Powerful Strategies That Move Customers To Make Fast, Favorable Decisions**, which was named by HubSpot as one of the 20 highest-rated sales books of all time; and, the award-winning **Zero-Time Selling: 10 Essential Steps to Accelerate Every Company's Sales**, which was recognized by Top Sales World as one of the Top 3 Sales & Marketing books of 2011. He is ranked #7 on Forbes list of the Top 30 global experts on social selling.

Andy is the founder of Zero-Time Selling, Inc., a sales advisory firm that is headquartered in San Diego (with offices in New York City.) Email: andy@andypaul.com, Twitter: @zerotimeselling

SALES HACK #20
MANUFACTURE SELLING TIME

A certain amount of non-selling time for your more efficient salespeople is inevitable. But for most salespeople and organizations, there's still plenty of opportunity to tighten up processes, workflow and general productivity in a finite amount of time to increase the percentage of the day & week your best reps are spending in front of customers and prospects.

Think about the difference between 55 and 65 percent active selling time across a 100+ person inside sales team. Just that 10-point improvement could mean significant additional sales without impacting cost, lead requirements or other expenditures.

How do you get there? Every selling environment is different, but these 10 opportunities are relatively universal.

1. **Batch admin work.** Don't get in the habit of making a call, leaving a voicemail, then disrupting your phone time to record the conversation in CRM, send a follow-up email, etc. Batch work items together to get and keep yourself in a groove. For example, make 10 calls all at once.

Keep notes on a pad of paper for any unique follow-ups. Then do all of your CRM and follow-up work at once. This batching of activities is proven to be faster and more efficient than doing everything in a linear sequence over and over and over again.

2. **Automate parallel or redundant tasks.** For example, every Salesforce.com user has a unique email address assigned to them. If you blind-copy yourself with that email address on any outbound email to a customer or prospect, it'll automatically record that email as an activity in the contact or lead's record. No need to go in and mark that separately. Anywhere you can automate activity on parallel tracks, you save steps and save time.

3. **Automate buying signal and trigger event alerts.** Driving efficiency on your floor is about more than cutting or eliminating steps and tasks. It's also driven by automating the filtering, highlighting and execution of prospect touch-points that are more likely to generate a response and conversation. Every day, there are buying signals and trigger events among your prospects and customers worth following up on. But rather than search through your social channels for hours on end, set up a series of alerts via LinkedIn, Newsle, OFunnel and more to bring those alerts right to your inbox. Dedicate time each day (first thing in the morning is ideal) to process through these alerts, thereby increasing the likelihood that you get a response later that same day.

4. **Develop and follow a prospect/account research process.** Do you leave your sales reps to their own devices to research a prospect before a meeting or call? How much time should this take anyway? Create a standardized system or process and you'll increase both consistency and success of these efforts while significantly reducing the time it takes to complete. For example, design a three-minute process for each rep to follow prior to any new prospect call. Have them check LinkedIn profiles, do a quick Google search, etc. to identify a specific set of information to leverage in the call – as an ice-breaker, to begin a consultative conversation, etc. Train the team on how to do this quickly, cleanly and efficiently. This alone could cut up to an hour a day of non-selling time for some of your reps.

5. **Invest in better tools (penny wise, quota foolish).** Don't be penny-wise but quota-foolish when it comes to tools investments. Think about that increase in sales output for the 10-point productivity gain referenced above. What would you spend to get there? Take Velocify, for example, which could help your sales reps more quickly decide who

to call next. How much time do your reps currently waste deciding who to call? And what if they decide to call someone that's not as ready for that call, and that decreases their connect and success rates? All of a sudden, that tool investment looks mighty attractive.

6. **Fewer victory laps**. This can be hard to enforce, but a disciplined sales rep can save themselves a ton of time by simply staying in their seat and moving to the next task. Breaks are fine, but we've all seen reps get an ounce of momentum on the phone, then get up and refresh coffee, flirt with the receptionist, etc. Encourage your reps to stay in the zone longer, and establish some rewards at the end if necessary.

7. **Better leads**. Not more leads. Better leads. More leads might mean the reps are calling prospects who aren't ready to buy. Their dials and talk time might increase, but their conversion rates will suffer. Many sales organizations see dramatic increases in productivity and output by delivering fewer leads to the sales team, but ensuring that those leads are qualified and ready for the conversation.

8. **Invest in great sales operations teams**. We've written about this before, but it bears repeating that a great sales operations can be the most important investment in sales productivity you can make. Read more about why we think that at http://www.heinzmarketing.com/2012/05/8-ways-sales-operations-can-double-your-teams-productivity/

9. **Improve the organization and availability of good content**. How much time does your sales team waste looking for the right piece of content to get to their prospect based on their unique stage of the buying process? When they find it, is it the most accurate and up to date content? Does your team know which piece of content (or type of content) is most appropriate for each prospect at each stage? Enormous efficiency gain potential here.

10. **Structure meeting time better**. This applies to both 1:1 meetings with your reps as well as group meetings. In your 1:1 time, have a specific agenda and keep your time focused. If you complete the agenda early and there's nothing left to discuss, give everybody their time back. In group meetings, have an agenda as well and ensure that what's covered is relevant to as many people in the room as possible. Pipeline reviews for example can be highly inefficient for the rest of the room if all you're doing is focusing on one rep's pipeline at a time with little to no value for the rest of the room.

What would you add to this list? What have you seen particularly drain productivity from your sales team, or work well to increase their active selling time?

Sales Hack contributed by: Matt Heinz, President, Heinz Marketing

Matt has more than 15 years of marketing, business development and sales

 experience from a variety of organizations, vertical industries and company sizes. Career has focused on delivering measurable results for his employers and clients in the way of greater sales, revenue growth, product success and customer loyalty.

Matt has held various positions at companies such as Microsoft, Weber Shandwick, Boeing, The Seattle Mariners, Market Leader and Verdiem. In 2007, began Heinz Marketing to help clients focus their business on market and customer opportunities, then execute a plan to scale revenue and customer growth.

SALES HACK #21
B2B SALES IS BUILT ON A LIE..
ENABLE CONSENSUS

The math behind selling through sales champions just doesn't add up.

Think about how long it takes your company to fully train and on-board a new sales rep. Let's say it takes three months—best case. That's a three-month investment before that rep is ready to close a sales opportunity on their own.

Once that rep is up to speed, they'll typically spend an hour or so educating the initial contact at a prospect company about your value proposition. Traditionally, after that first hour, the rep is reliant on that individual contact to identify and teach the other stakeholders in their company. This risky approach effectively turns that individual contact into a "sales champion", making them responsible for getting the other influencers, stakeholders, users, and decision makers on board with the idea of buying your solution.

Stepping back for a moment, we can see that this formula doesn't make sense. If it takes at least three months to train a new sales rep before they can handle meaningful business opportunities, why would you entrust someone who's spent just one hour learning about a product or service with the responsibility of selling it to their colleagues—each of whom may bring a different functional view and possibly geographic priority to the conversation.

A lot can go wrong when you entrust your sales message to a barely-informed messenger. The story can go south: they can mix up the value proposition and kill the deal before it's really even begun. The prospect may not be able to overcome their peers' objections effectively, or drive all stakeholders to a consensus.

The research backs this up. Data from CEB shows that when you move from selling to one person to selling to a group of two people, purchase likelihood drops from 81 percent to 55 percent. By the time you reach the B2B sales average of 5.4 decision makers, purchase likelihood drops to 31 percent - that's a 61 percent drop!

So the sales champion—the individual with whom a rep has spent just an hour or so—is faced with an incredible challenge: they must somehow find a way to convince the other stakeholders in their company's buying group that your solution is the right one. Clearly, a one-hour training session doesn't equip someone to fully understand your value proposition, let alone adapt it to the unique needs of a variety of people who might each represent a different area of the customer's business. And the complexity of a purchasing decision can quickly multiply, especially in large organizations where deals can involve multiple divisions and locations.

The 31 percent likelihood I mention above looks eerily similar to the industry average for sales close rates. The B2B sales industry is built on a foundation of sand, relying on ill-equipped sales champions to drive consensus among groups of stakeholders. In fact, sales acceleration and marketing automation tools are nearly all designed to connect and engage sellers with individual sales champions, reinforcing the problem behavior.

What's been missing is the answer to a key question: how can we enable the B2B buying group as a whole to make fast, confident purchasing decisions? This question is at the heart of this sales hack.

You MUST enable B2B buying groups to make fast and confident purchase decisions if you hope to break through your current close rate. Start by equipping sales champions to share relevant sales messaging with each member of the buying committee, personalized to their persona.

Left on their own, a sales champion will do her best to explain your value proposition to other stakeholders, but different users, managers, decision makers, budget controllers—and even the sales champion—can easily misinterpret your story and the value of what you offer.

You should create assets (Videos, PDFs, Infographics, Decks, etc.) that speak specifically to each individual stakeholder (all the way down to the user level), and train your sales team to equip their "sales champion" to share those assets with the right people in their efforts to drive consensus. Strategic buyers should receive high level use case, ROI, required work, and value-metric information. Budget controllers should see ROI and pricing detail. Users should see user-level use cases and individual value metric messaging. Understand the buyer persona of each unique stakeholder in your buying groups, give them relevant messaging (directly or through your champion), and you'll see your close rate jump, maybe even dramatically.

Relying on sales champions clearly doesn't add up. The question is, what are you going to do about it?

Sales Hack contributed by: Matt Behrend, Co-Founder & Chief Sales Officer, DemoChimp

Matt is wired for entrepreneurship and business building. He has passion  for building and maintaining high product/market fit and developing growth systems around it. Matt believes none of that can happen without strong relationships that are built on integrity, authenticity and creative execution. Basically, Matt loves building and growing cool stuff with great people - and learning everything I can along the way.

SALES HACK #22
THE CONTENT HACK

One of my favorite current "hacks" is content selling. Content selling is the practice of leveraging content to support sales as they facilitate the buyer's progression through their buying process. Sales is trained to understand who the buyer is, where they are in the process, and what they need. Once they understand those factors, they use content, along with some strategically designed sales plays, to help move the buyer along. This approach is fundamentally different from the standard "close-close-close" approach and it works. Greg Alexander from Sales Benchmark Index has said on numerous occasions: "In the future, a piece of great content will outsell an average sales rep. The self-directed buyer will begin to make complex purchases with zero rep involvement. Scary for some. Exciting for others."

One of my favorite content selling plays is called the champion content play. Champion content is content designed specifically for your internal champion who is interested in your solution but must navigate his/her own organization to help advance the deal.

Here is how it works: Champion content is provided to your internal champion to help them sell your project internally. Many sales organizations are aware of the situation: "Our champion likes what they have heard and are bought in". The process looks like it is moving forward so the sales rep moves them to 40-60% in the pipeline. What is happening on the buyer side is another story. Your champion now needs to maneuver internally and there are many potential roadblocks that stand in the way of the process. For example, the champion will need to get buy-off from a number of different stakeholders. There is a minimum of 3-5 stakeholders that will influence your purchase and depending on your solution. There might also be multiple departments, multiple people, and more importantly, competing agendas. Sales people often lose visibility into the deal at this point and in many cases, deals will stall or the buyer will drop out.

For many sales organizations, the predominant issue is the buying committee or other stakeholders in the process, but your solution might have other potential roadblocks like infrastructure, regulatory, or compatibility issues. The goal is to get in front of the process and create champion content to help buyers more effectively and efficiently resolve these issues on their end.

Here is an example: The Champion Deck. The Champion Deck is one of the best examples of content selling play. Steve Hays, CEO of Insidesalesteam.com, helps his champions overcome internal resistance with "the champion deck". His sales process typically starts with a champion who then needs to sell the idea to other stakeholders in the organization. In order to help their champions navigate internally, they created a champion deck. The champion deck includes the following:

- A real-world, "no-brainer" ROI model for everyone.
- Real customer data — If they can use the buyer's real numbers, they will insert them into the deck.
- Comparisons to other alternatives including competitors and in-house alternatives. If they can include alternatives they know the buyer has already evaluated, they will insert them into the deck.
- Relevant case studies of similar companies to the buyers.

The champion can then use this deck to help sell internally.

As more organizations embrace a buyer-centric approach and lean heavily on content, we will see more examples of content selling helping accelerate pipelines and win deals. Stay tuned on the TOPO blog as we continue to write about more use cases across the entire buying process and provide more examples of content selling in action.

Sales Hack contributed by: Craig Rosenberg, Chief Analyst and Co-Founder of TOPO

Craig Rosenberg is the Chief Analyst and Co-founder of TOPO, a research and advisory firm that helps sales and marketing organizations adopt the patterns and plays used by the world's fastest growing companies. Craig is also well-known for his work as the editor of the very popular sales and marketing blog, the Funnelholic.

SALES HACK #23
HACK YOUR MINDSET TO BOOST SALES

The single most important element that will determine how far we go in life is our mindset.

Our mindset is a set of attitudes and beliefs that influence and shape our behaviors. According to scientific researchers, we start to create these attitudes and beliefs the moment we're born. We store them in a particular area of our brain, called the prefrontal cortex. This is where neural connections form into cognitive elements, memories, and associated feelings from past experiences. Some call this the executive function of the brain — I like to think of the prefrontal cortex as our "inner CEO."

Professor Michael Bernard at the University of Melbourne, Australia has studied high performing people at work. His research uncovered which specific beliefs and behaviors create a high performance mindset. These high achievers consciously create a belief system that helps them cope effectively with difficult situations. They're also able to identify and eliminate the performance blockers that might stand in the way of their success.

We can see these traits in great leaders. Take Bill McDermott, a former Xerox account rep who is now the CEO of SAP, a company with a $90 billion market cap. When he worked at Xerox, he took over Puerto Rico – the worst performing territory in the country – and moved it to first place within 12 months simply by changing the team's mindset. When he published his book, *Winners Dream,* he gave a speech at a private reception in New York, which I recorded so I could analyze his magical ability to connect with people through authenticity, humility, and confidence. He displayed all the behavioral characteristics described in Dr. Bernard's research.

Our mindset is also the key to unlock our physical performance. For example, Dr. Becca Levy at Yale University found that when people over 50 years of age create a positive mindset about aging, they would actually live 7.6 years longer than people with a mindset that's negative. So, if you hold the belief in your prefrontal cortex that age is a matter of progressive deterioration, chances are that your body will shut down 7.6 years earlier.

Another example of a person with a high performance mindset is Dan

Waldschmidt, author of *Edgy Conversation*. He recently ran a 100-mile race (nearly the equivalent of four consecutive marathons) and finished first, beating more than 150 people (only 10% of the runners actually finished the race). Dan uses two high-performance coaches that help him with his mind-body connection to get his body to achieve progressively greater results.

When I asked Dan about what led to his win, he mentioned how he stumbled over a root early into the race, injuring three of his toes. To overcome this setback, he focused his mindset on winning; his mantra was "never stop running." He admitted to experiencing negative self-talk at the early stages of the race. He asked himself, "Why am I doing this?" or "Why did I get up at 5 a.m. to compete?" He edited his self-talk and didn't let negative thoughts overtake his focus. Dr. Bernard calls this quality "high self-regard." The instant Dan's mind drifts into a negative mode, he corrects it.

In fact, when Dan wakes up in the morning, he begins the day with positive affirmation: "Today I will do whatever it takes, for as long as it takes, to achieve my goals." Dan also meditates every day to clear his mind and connect with his true self. When the going gets tough, he, Dan, says to himself, "Every day in every way I am getter better and better by the choices I make and the actions I take."

Research shows that our mindset is under constant assault by an avalanche of negativity. Think about your day at work. How many thoughts did you experience? An NIH study recently revealed that on a typical day we experience about 60,000 thoughts. Here is the interesting fact: 80%, or 48,000 of our thoughts are negative.

The good news is that we can learn how to edit our response to negative thoughts, choose to act positively, and direct our minds to become a powerful, positive, and productive force. When you feel you possess the executive power to be the writer, actor, and director of your own life, you've achieved a peak-performance mindset. Here are a few hacks to do just that.

1. Make a deep commitment to reach your goals. Before committing to a goal, high performers ask themselves: "How big is my why?" and "How strong is my try?" Average performers make a commitment only in their minds, which means they will lose it the moment they encounter resistance. Top performers make a commitment in their hearts as well as their minds, which means no adversity will be strong

enough to hold them back.

Average performers show a great deal of interest in setting goals and achieving them. High performers take this to the next level and transform their interest into a deep commitment. They know that life doesn't get better because of your interests; it gets better because of your commitments.

a) Connect your goal with your heart and soul. If you don't love the outcome, it won't change your income.
b) Connect your goal to your dreams – there is nothing more powerful and meaningful than turning a dream into reality.
c) Tell three people close to you about your goal; explain why it is important for you to reach this goal, and ask them to support you.
d) Create your own "wall of dreams." Cut out pictures of your dream house, your dream vacation, your dream car, your dream charity, or your dream family and paste them on your wall for everyone to see. Chart your progress every week.

2. Create the confidence you need to succeed High sales achievers create positive energy through their decision, their actions and their physiology. Start your journey to success by simply declaring that you will be victorious. Next, visualize your actions step by step.

If you find that you need more energy, stand up, raise both arms over your head, and stand for two minutes in the "victory" position. It is a scientifically proven fact that within two minutes your testosterone levels will go up and your cortisol levels will go down. You'll feel more energized and calm and ready to act with determination and purpose.

3. Make a deeper commitment to others. High performers win by helping other people win. In the past we moved from dependence to independence; today, technology has helped us move towards interdependence. Every person on this earth plays a part in building a better world. It all starts with a mindset that's connected to the heart. In fact, Dr. Gary Hamel at Stanford University suggested in a recent speech that we successful leaders are moving from pragmatism to love.

4. Don't fake your commitment to success. It's not good enough to say, "I'll do whatever it takes, for as long as it takes, to reach my goals." You need to back it up with authentic action. Don't let your rational mind fool you into thinking that you can take a break from your commitments. Monitor your self-sabotaging thoughts and don't let

them rob you of your chances for reaching peak performance.

Sales Hack contributed by: Gerhard Gschwandtner, CEO & Founder, Selling Power

My personal mantra is "excellence is a question of expanding awareness". When all is said and done, I am a sales guy. I established my professional

reputation as a sales guru by training over 10,000 salespeople in Europe and the US. I realized that salespeople and their managers need all the help they can get; that's why I started Selling Power magazine and turned it into the world's leading sales management magazine. My mission is to contribute to the success of sales leaders with SellingPower.com, a sales intelligence platform that's visited by over 300,000 sales leaders every month.

SALES HACK #24
LEADERS ARE READERS

Student: I know what I like.

Master: You like what you know.

Before you barrel through the following list of books, take a deep breath.

Most of us will scroll right to the list, hastily scanning the titles with an "Oh, I know that one...that one, too...hmm, never heard of it...*that* one's good."

Slow your roll.

We're all used to tweets and texts, and flying through content. Books, however, require focus and attention. So peruse this list and consider how each book might improve your approach to problems, or work, or people. Think about *buying* each book.

Become a student.

If you *truly* want to be a better leader, better salesperson, better speaker, better writer, or just a better person, you need to **study** the craft. And if you look hard, you'll find there's already a book with the instructions.

Make the best use of your limited time. It's not like you need the home study, the leather chair, or the warm reading lamp over your shoulder for "reading time."
- Listen to audiobooks on your commute.
- Subscribe to your favorite blogs and have articles emailed to you.
- Discover awesome subjects by joining Goodreads.
- Hear what others inquire about on Quora.
- Join the discussions on LinkedIn Groups.
- Read cool stories in minutes on Medium.

Leaders are readers. Studies continue to find that most CEO's read 4-5 books a month and earn 350% more income than the average American. So don't take this list with a grain of salt. Get under the hood and explore all these books have to offer.

Work on yourself harder than you work on your job. If you stay ready, you won't need to get ready. You stay ready by reading.

These books are listed in no particular order, and I'm not encouraged or paid to recommend them. They also don't represent ALL the ones I'd suggest. It's all out there, though, part of a slew of great lists that will recommend excellent titles for you. Remember, what you seek is seeking you.

#1 *Thinkertoys* by Michael Michalko - Find two solutions to every problem you encounter. It'll get you thinking and acting like a leader. And you'll be surprised how often you can resolve issues on your own. Buy *Thinkertoys* here: bit.ly/thinkertoys

#2 *The 10X Rule* by Grant Cardone - How much money did you make in the last 24 hours? If you want a better-than-average anything in life, then you need to think and act better-than-average. Stop telling yourself why you can't achieve greatness and limiting your beliefs. Buy *The 10X Rule* here: bit.ly/10XRule-

#3 *Wooden on Leadership* by John Wooden - If every player on the team plays to the best of their ability, the team won't need to look at the scoreboard or talk about winning. The late UCLA Basketball Coach, John Wooden, inspired his team to win 10 NCAA national titles in a 12-year span. Coach Wooden's legacy was built on his Pyramid of Success, which he explains in great detail. Speaking of detail, Coach Wooden once said, "It's the little details that are vital. Little things make big things happen." Buy *Wooden On Leadership* here: bit.ly/Wooden-

#4 *How to Win Friends and Influence People* by Dale Carnegie - If everyone practiced the lessons in this book, the world would be a better place. Dale Carnegie wrote it in 1936, and it remains applicable to today's world. "Become genuinely interested in other people," "Begin in a friendly way," and "Praise every improvement" are just a few of Carnegie's teachings. If you change, everything will change for you. Reading this book is your first step. Buy *How to Win Friends and Influence People* here: bit.ly/win_friends

#5 *The Sales Acceleration Formula* by Mark Roberge - Sales leader Mark Roberge reveals the framework and formula behind HubSpot's incredible scaling efforts. These very practices propelled HubSpot into the public market's open arms. Like famous equations that changed the world, *this* formula teaches you how the power of inbound lead generation, marketing and sales data, pipeline and activity metrics, and sales technology can change your business for the better. Buy *The Sales Acceleration Formula* here: bit.ly/roberge-sales

#6 *The Little Red Book of Selling* by Jeffrey Gitomer - It doesn't matter what Gitomer book you read, you'll learn better ways to sell. This one happens to be the one I've referred to the most. Jeffrey's style of writing, his tone, and his tips can't be ignored – value oozes from them. Similar to Jill Konrath (see #10), I've subscribed to Jeffrey Gitomer's free eNewsletter, *Sales Caffeine* for YEARS (about ten now). This particular book is the largest-selling sales book of all time, worldwide. Buy *Little Red Book of Selling* here: bit.ly/lil_red

#7 *Predictable Revenue* by Aaron Ross, Marylou Tyler - Known by many as "the bible" of SaaS sales development, this book provides a bevy of proven ideas for managing the top of the funnel. Aaron unveils proven best practices created and used by Salesforce.com. It's a guide that remains relevant, by many standards, and is a must-read for anyone in demand generation and sales development.
Buy *Predictable Revenue* here: bit.ly/predict-rev

#8 *Think and Grow Rich* by Napoleon Hill - Wouldn't you agree you will acquire knowledge by reading all the books on this list (or even half of them)? All that knowledge won't be worth jack – nor will it attract the income you're likely after – without practical PLANS OF ACTION. This book was published one year after Dale Carnegie's (see #4) – like, um, EIGHTY years ago. Apply what you learn from it, right here and now, in our world of SaaS, social media, texts, tweets, and eMedia, and elevate yourself, your company, your product, your brand, and your customers to unthinkable heights. Buy *Think and Grow Rich* here: bit.ly/thinkngrow-rich

#9 *Jab, Jab, Jab, Right Hook* by Gary Vaynerchuk - Though it might be the same story, you'll need to tell it differently to a group of executives vs. a group of your friends. The term means to give, give, give, and then ask. "Gary Vee" explains, in great detail, how to do this online, and includes methods for telling your story on every major social media platform. If you're looking to build your brand, then you'll want to know how to "speak the language" of each channel, and each audience. Buy *Jab, Jab, Jab, Right Hook* here: bit.ly/gv-jjjrh

#10 *Agile Selling* by Jill Konrath - I have followed Jill Konrath since 2007, when I subscribed to her "Selling to Big Companies" blog. To this day, she sheds value on the sales industry like a bright, warm sunshine.

Buy *Agile Selling* here: bit.ly/konrath-agile

#11 *The Ultimate Sales Machine* by Chet Holmes - I've read this book a good 20 times, and have referred to it throughout my sales leadership career. It offers a 12-part program only used by high-caliber sales organizations, and requires "pig-headed discipline and determination" to work. Buy *The Ultimate Sales Machine* here: bit.ly/UltimateSales-

#12 *The New Solution Selling* by Keith M. Eades - To know where you're going means you need to know where you came from. This is the update to Mike Bosworth's early 90's classic, *Solution Selling*. Applying a sales methodology to your selling gives you a tried and true advantage, and enables you to plan your work and work your plan. Among the popular methodologies, this happens to be a favorite. It uses the formula PPVVC=S (Pain x Power x Vision x Value x Control = Sale) to help salespeople accurately gauge the probability of closing a deal. Buy *The New Solution Selling* here: bit.ly/new-solution

#13 *The First 90 Days* by Michael Watkins - This book is a roadmap for leaders starting in a new organization. Time is critical in the first 90 days, and the faster you can reach "the breakeven point," where you become a contributor of value vs. a consumer of value, the better. Watkins provides real-world scenarios, several potential approaches, and different types of dialogue, to help you anticipate and prepare for any situation in your new environment. Buy *The First 90 Days* here: bit.ly/First90-

#14 *Difficult Conversations* by Douglas Stone, Bruce Patton - It's inevitable. You're going to have difficult conversations – with senior leaders, with sales reps, with prospects and customers. Of course, most of us want to prevent these talks, or avoid them altogether. When you're focused, however, on productive problem solving instead of emotion or "winning" the argument, you're able to calmly arrive with your "opponent" at a path forward. This book lays out the best, most professional, tactful, and respectful ways to handle difficult conversations. Buy *Difficult Conversations* here: bit.ly/diff-convo

#15 *Smart Calling* by Art Sobczak - Many argue that "cold calling" is dead, and in many ways it is. "Calling," however, is alive and well, and salespeople NEED to know how to conduct a great phone call. Sales trainer and coach, Art Sobczak, shares "dumb mistakes" most salespeople say in the first 10 seconds of their calls; and offers new, better approaches to ensure you engage people on the phone vs. spilling info about you, your company, and your product all over them. Buy *Smart*

Calling here: bit.ly/smart-calling

#16 *Money – Master the Game* by Tony Robbins - Assuming you're going to crush it in your sales career, you'll make a lot of money. You better learn how to manage it or it will disappear. It was once said, "If you took all the money in the world, divided it up equally among everybody, it would soon all be back in the same pockets." Tony Robbins spells out 7 simple steps to financial freedom, and interviews the world's money masters, so you can model their success for yourself. Buy *Money – Master the Game* here: bit.ly/robbins-money

#17 *The 7 Habits of Highly Effective People* by Stephen Covey - I attended a leadership conference in the early 2000's, and Dr. Covey was the keynote speaker. He had us stand up, cover our eyes, and point to where we thought was north. He then asked everyone to keep pointing while they uncovered their eyes. Everyone was pointing in a different direction. In order to influence an organization of any size to head in the same direction, everyone must develop fundamental habits – like seeking first to understand before you're understood. Buy *The 7 Habits of Highly Effective People* here: bit.ly/7-habits-

#18 *Jack: Straight from the Gut* by Jack Welch, John A. Byrne - Jack Welch is a master at business leadership. By driving culture before anything else, he shaped GE to become the "most valuable company in the world." This book illustrates Jack's career path, his candid view on what matters most to businesses, his succession plan for up-and-coming executives (including personal, handwritten letters to his leaders), and the deep dives he encourages us to take when working on *our* business. Buy *Jack: Straight from the Gut* here: bit.ly/jack-ceo

#19 *The Psychology of Selling* by Brian Tracy - "Get serious about your career; decide today to be a big success in everything you do." This quote from Brian Tracy is the first of my five philosophies, and a staple of my daily work. Here, Brian walks through strategies and methods for moving deals through the pipeline and adding more "Closed Won" deals to the board. It is a classic book you'll reference throughout your career. Buy *The Psychology of Selling* here: bit.ly/psych-selling

#20 *Overcoming The Five Dysfunctions of a Team* by Patrick Lencioni - If you're part of a struggling company or team, it's likely because one or more of these dysfunctions is at play: absence of trust, fear of conflict, lack of commitment, avoidance of accountability, or inattention to results. This is one of TEN powerhouse business and sales books from Pat Lencioni. Buy *Overcoming the Five Dysfunctions of a Team* here: bit.ly/5-dysfunctions

#21 *Zig Ziglar's Secrets of Closing the Sale* by Zig Ziglar - The man. Zig Ziglar is a sales legend, and his lessons continue to resonate today. I never took the opportunity to see him live, but still listen to and watch his teachings. In this book, Zig underscores the fact that "we're all in sales." He breaks down the very questions, attitude, and steps required to influence a "Yes!" from people. Buy *Zig Ziglar's Secrets of Closing the Sale* here: bit.ly/zigsecrets

#22 *21.5 Unbreakable Laws of Selling* by Jeffrey Gitomer - It doesn't matter what Gitomer book you read, you'll learn better ways to sell. This one happens to be the one I've referred to the most. Buy *21.5 Unbreakable Laws of Selling* here: bit.ly/git21-5

#23 *Execution: The Discipline of Getting Things Done* by Ram Charan, Larry Bossidy - The title mentions "the discipline of getting things done." That alone should inspire you to read this book. Ram Charan is a business legend, and has advised the greatest CEO's of all time, while Larry Bossidy has led at incredibly successful companies like Honeywell and GE. Buy *Execution: The Discipline of Getting Things Done* here: bit.ly/Execution-

They're not all here. WAY more books (and best sales books lists) are out there, containing ALL the answers you need to succeed. Schedule time to crack them open, and become the awesome salesperson you are. This was a peek at my bookshelf. These books, without question, will bolster your self-improvement, develop your leadership presence, guide you towards building effective teams, offer you different ways of solving problems, and show you how to do your job better.

Sales Hack contributed by: Ralph Barsi, Vice President, Field Operations

I serve businesses and people, by helping both become better than they were when I arrived. For businesses: I've created and overseen scalable, repeatable, sales, inside sales, and operations organizations that produce – framing the strategy, finding the best people, designing the process, and leveraging effective technology. My efforts have resulted in millions of dollars in revenue pipeline and closed deals.

For people: I've coached, mentored, and inspired professionals to reach the highest levels in their career. The talent pipelines I've built have shaped training grounds and driven internal promotions. I believe people should work where they're celebrated, not tolerated; and I'm proud of the alumni group of direct reports I've developed over the years.

SALES HACK #25
GET 1 PERCENT BETTER EVERY DAY

I am <u>not</u> the greatest salesperson in the world. If you don't believe me, ask Dave Kurlan, CEO of Objective Management Group. The OMG assessment that I personally took along with my sales team pointed out my strengths, weaknesses, and areas of opportunity—which was great because it allowed me to understand my weak points, and focus on improving in those areas.

The two traits that I am strong in, according the Objective Management Group Sales Assessment, happen to be the most important leading indicators of sales success.

- ✓ **Trainable and Coachable**
- ✓ **Strong Desire for Sales Success**

The biggest area of improvement based on the OMG Sales Assessment:

- ✓ **Don't get emotional**

The Ultimate Sales Hack

Discover your strengths and weaknesses early in your career by assessing your sales traits using the Objective Management Group Sales Assessment so that you can understand your strengths, and your personal weak spots and turn your weaknesses into your strengths.

The Impact

The impact of knowing if you have what it takes to be successful in sales (or not) enables you to be the best sales professional that you can be by learning from others.

At 211 degrees, water is hot.

At 212 degrees, it boils.

And with boiling water, comes steam. And steam can power a locomotive.

One extra degree... makes all the difference. And, the one extra degree of effort in business and in life... separates the good from the great! From the book *212 Degrees, The Extra Degree*, by Sam Parker

Put another way, if you focus on getting just 1 percent better every single day, at the end of a year, you will be 250% better then you were on day one. Think of it this way, are you a better sales person today, or the day you were born.

A quote from Kraig Kleeman that always sticks with me, "I would rather choke on greatness than settle for mediocrity."

How does one execute The Ultimate Sales Hack?

Step 1: Visit http://www.objectivemanagement.com/omginfo/page/Contact.aspx to learn more about the sales assessment.

Step 2: Schedule time with a regional Objective Management Group consultant to review your results.

Step 3: Take action! If you discover that you have "the money gap" or any other sales gaps after taking the assessment, do something about it.

Once you recognize your gaps, then what?

There are several things that you can do to improve your skills in sales. Perhaps the number one thing you can do, as Stephen D'Angelo shared with me long ago, is more sales transactions. By being involved in sales transactions, you will naturally learn how to sell better. Here are five specific actions you can take to improve:

1. **Join a sales association in your area.** There are several of these including, The American Association of Inside Sales Professionals. If you are located in the Bay Area, consider The Inside Sales Leadership Alliance (https://www.linkedin.com/groups/Inside-Sales-Leadership-Alliance-1418447/about). If you Google "sales association" in your region, there are plenty to choose from.
2. **Attend a sales training workshop.** Many of the authors in this book also host regular sales boot camps. For example, Skip Miller, CEO of

M3Learning, puts on a sales training program in Saratoga, California every quarter (http://m3learning.wpengine.com/programs/sales-reps/) and Dave Kurlan hosts regular sales and sales leadership training events in Massachusetts (visit www.kurlanassociates.com).

3. **Find a mentor.** Not all sales leaders are created equal. Once you've found out your strengths and weaknesses, "interview" your prospective manager before going to work for them. What sales training methodology do they adhere to? Have they had a successful track record in sales? What do people who work for them say about the person? Pick your mentors wisely and then share your results from your assessment with them. If they don't know your weak spots, how can they help you grow in your sales career?

4. **Network, network, network.** Every sales author/leader in this book has different experiences and different insights that they could share that could make you a better sales professional. Without being exposed to greatness, it is difficult to become great. So attend trade shows, connect with people on LinkedIn and ask your manager for introductions to the people he looks up to.

5. **Read.** My book case is packed full of sales books from Og Mandino, author of *The Greatest Salesman In the World*, to *The Art of War For Salespeople*, by Sun Tzu, and hundreds more. Ask your mentor, ask your sales colleagues, ask the authors of this book, and you will get pointed to many books that can help you take your sales career to the next level of professionalism and performance.

The Ultimate Sales Hack is not a quick fix to sales success. It is however, the best way that I have found to improve your sales skills daily/weekly/monthly to always try to be the best sales professional that you can be.

Chad Burmeister, Vice President of Sales & Marketing, ConnectAndSell (Twitter handle: @SalesHack)

Chad has been voted as a Top 25 Most Influential Inside Sales Professional

 by the American Association of Inside Sales Professionals 6 years in a row – 2010, 2011, 2012, 2013, 2014, and 2015.

THE 8 BONUS SALES HACKS

BONUS SALES HACK #1
START WITH THE PUNCHLINE

Sales people spend (read "waste") precious time during prospecting calls. Given the short window to engage the prospect and change the nature of the call from an "interruption" to a sales "conversation", it's crucial we maximize those precious early seconds at the start of the call. But when you listen to most B2B reps tele-prospecting, they regularly squander these valuables seconds.

Give them the punch line first.

Don't start with who you are, the company you work for, what you do or how, and all that other stuff that no one outside your company walls cares about; all the while failing give the buyer anything remotely in it for them. Start with the very last thing in your current talk track first.

That's right. Scrap the rest, or at a minimum turn it upside down, but give them the ending – the outcome – the impact on their business – right at the start.

Start with the punch line, leave everything for after that, or completely out.

Ask yourself, what was the prospect thinking about before they picked up the phone? Who you are and what you do? Or how they will achieve their objective, the outcomes they desire, the specific impact on their business? Give them the impact you have delivered for others, and worry about the rest later. Give them the punch line first.

Tibor Shanto has been a sales leader for over 25 years, helping companies  improve their revenue goals. He is a sought-after trainer, speaker and co-author of the award winning book Shift!: Harness The Trigger Events That Turn Prospects Into Customers. He is a columnist for the Globe & Mail Report on Small Business. Tibor was ranked 8th on the list of The World's Top Social Sellers, as presented on Forbes.com. His received the Gold Medal Top Sales & Marketing Blog award in 2013, and was named OpenView's Top 25 Sales Influencers in 2014, as well as Top Sales' Top 50 Sales & Marketing Influencers for 2013, 2014 and 2015.

BONUS SALES HACK #2
THE "32 SECOND" HACK

"This is (Sales Rep) with (Company). I realize I am an interruption. Do you have (unique # of seconds, I use 32) so I can tell you why I am calling?"

There are three separate parts to why this introduction works as it slowly breaks down the Decision Maker's guard.

The first part is recognizing you are interrupting someone's day. No one is sitting at their desk waiting for your call. Speaking to this fact is simply relating to them and allowing them to feel like you understand them and their situation of being very busy.

The second part is the unique number, which is called a pattern interrupt. It is like someone coming up to you and asking what color you would paint a baby. It is an attention getter!

The third part has nothing to do with a pitch or value prop; you are simply asking if they are OK with you letting them know why you are calling.

All three of these pieces make it EXTREMELY difficult to say no to you as you aren't selling anything yet.

Sales Hack contributed by: Jourdan DuFort, Sr. Account Executive, ConnectAndSell

Jourdan is a Senior Account Executive for ConnectAndSell and entrepreneur who has a great knack for cold calling developed early in his

career starting a door-to-door sales company. He enjoys working with startups as it gives him the opportunity to be creative and learn in hyper- growth organizations. In just 2 years of being with ConnectAndSell he feels he has accelerated his career by 10 years because of how many business conversations ConnectAndSell's innovative technology delivers every day.

BONUS SALES HACK #3
KNOW YOUR BUSINESS

Many years ago, I learned a simple, yet valuable, lesson that has stayed with me and I feel is helpful whether you're an individual contributor, manager, director or executive.

Early in my career, I was hired as an Inside Sales Manager to establish and grow a new team. In one of my first meetings with my new boss, our VP of Sales, he explained he did not have a lot of time and he would not be available to "guide me". He stated that he had hired me because at my level he expected I would know "everything" already. He went on to tell me that I would be stretched and put in situations that I would have to figure out, and he expected I may make some mistakes, which he said was ok, but warned, "I better understand the reasons why…". In other words, he told me to "know my business."

I thought about that and realized as simple and obvious as it sounded, those words were powerful – **know your business**. But what does that mean and what is the impact?

Well, for me, I realized that if I truly understood what we're doing, why we're doing it, and how we're doing it (and I mean really understood it), then I could analyze the results and take appropriate actions. This was HUGE and I saw that it touched every aspect of my role, including how I interacted with my team and other internal individuals and departments, sales strategies and processes, tools, products, external conditions, and so much more.

His point was so clear: if I understand it and something isn't working, adjust and correct it. If something is working, replicate it.

The impact of this simple lesson can be significant and make a HUGE difference, but note that simple does not mean easy. To accomplish this, you must take time and drill deep to develop a thorough understanding of the various aspects of your activities and the associated results.

So ask yourself, how well do you know your business?

Sales Hack contributed by: Larry Reeves, CEO, The American Association of Inside Sales Professionals

With over 30 years sales and marketing experience, Larry Reeves brings a multidimensional perspective to the AA-ISP executive team. He has managed virtually every aspect of the inside sales industry, from building high performing sales organizations to the strategic development of outsourcing and channel partnerships. Larry's diverse professional background includes inside sales leadership positions with high tech manufacturers and integrators Silicon Graphics and Unisys. He's held executive leadership roles with the outsourcers Sutherland Group and Performark. An exceptional team builder and motivator, Larry has developed a well-earned reputation for his operational expertise and ability to improve efficiency and productivity. He is a recognized authority in performance tracking and management, CRM tools and data management, and sales and marketing programs. Larry holds a Bachelor of Science degree in Management Information Systems from St. John Fisher College, Rochester, New York.

AA-ISP

BONUS SALES HACK #4
FLIP THE CUP

Most sales managers don't really believe they can do anything to help their sales reps change their behavior. NOT TRUE! The sales leader of a Fortune 500 software company introduced me to a low-tech sales hack that drives new sales behaviors and resets client expectations.

It's called "Flip the Cup", but it's no drinking game. During the last week of each month, every salesperson on the team is required to successfully make contact with every one of their clients and active prospects with one objective: to source, accelerate or close opportunities. The first three days of the week are spent talking with customers; the last two are spent planning for next month.

When sales managers focus solely on outcomes (sales, gross margin, close rates, month-end targets) they create rep dysfunction, fear of failure, and resistance to change. It's not their intention, but it's the result.

Flip the Cup drives productive behaviors by refocusing sales teams on buyer engagement: connecting in meaningful ways with prospects and customers to understand needs, priorities, budgets, and decision-making processes.

For the same reason that "flip cup" is the ultimate drinking game, "Flip the Cup" is the ultimate sales hack. There is no limit on the number of people that can get involved, it requires no special equipment and all you need is great motivated people.

Flip the Cup today and watch your results improve next month!

Sales Hack contributed by: David DiStefano, Chief Revenue Officer, PeopleLinx

I am a C-suite executive and sales thought leader. I am passionate about working with sales leaders to identify critical success factors necessary to alter their status quo, and to develop transformative solutions that drive successful business outcomes. As its CEO, I led the transformation and significant growth of Richardson to its prominent position in the sales training space. In 2015, I joined the executive team of an exciting young company, PeopleLinx, to help scale this social sales enablement organization. Today I spend my time demonstrating to sales leaders the enormous value and opportunity of integrating social business channels into existing sales processes.

BONUS SALES HACK #5
THE SOCIAL SELLING WORKFLOW

In this day and age, any sales rep can have a social media presence and use social media networks to sell in the B2B space. Having worked on both sales and marketing teams, I've realized that to simply have strong social media presence and engaging inconsistently with your buyer is not a good enough indicator to predict the total number of sales opportunities and closed deals from social selling strategies.

In order to predict and measure social selling success, a detailed social selling cadence, tempo and/or workflow needs to exist.

Over the past three years, I've been able to work with 100+ inside sales reps to test multiple social selling workflows. After much trial, error and countless hours of testing, I've been able to prove and come up with a unique workflow which essentially integrates traditional prospecting strategies with new age social selling tactics to fill your pipeline and increase revenue. Here is how it works:

"Social Selling Revenue" Workflow – Created by Gabe Villamizar

1. 3x3 Buyer Research
2. LinkedIn Connect/LinkedIn InMail
3. Twitter Follow
4. Twitter Engagement
5. LinkedIn Engagement
6. Phone Call
7. Voicemail

So why does this social selling workflow work for outbound prospecting? I have a dozen obvious reasons and non-obvious reasons of why it works. If you think about it, if an SDR/BDR/ADM follows each of the steps outlined above, he or she will have successfully had 7 touch points with the buyer in less than a 24 hour period. Having said that, when was the last time you were to contact your buyer seven times within 24 hours by strictly cold calling and cold emailing them within 24 hours without pissing them off and screwing up the deal? This is exactly my point.

According CEB, 75% of B2B buyers now use social media to be informed on vendors. If this is the case, inside sales reps can't afford not to social sell on daily basis. Keep in mind that tracking every activity on

Salesforce.com is crucial in order to create a predictable social selling model. If you'd like to learn more about social selling and how to roll this out, check out my online course at http://www.embedsocialselling.com

Sales Hack contributed by: Gabe Villamizar, Social Media Marketing Manager

Gabe Villamizar (@GabeVillamizar) is recognized as a leading Social Selling Professional by Inc.com & Forbes. He's trained and coached 100+ inside sales reps on social selling in the B2B SaaS space. Gabe formerly worked with InsideSales.com and laid the foundation of their first social media, social selling and social thought leadership strategies along with Ken Krogue. He currently works for HireVue and consults companies to help them increase revenue through social selling and social media marketing.

BONUS SALES HACK #6
THE STRATEGIC ROAD MAP

Step one - Strategic road maps begin with understanding who you are as a company and making sure everyone shares, and can share, the same value proposition (Elevator Pitch). After all, if you cannot internalize your message, it's doubtful you can externalize your message.

Step two – Build personas based on your existing customers. This will help you understand your prospects pain points and how to develop a content strategy that converts more prospects into customers.

Step three – Develop a communication strategy for influencers (Media Executives, Analysts and Social Media Pundits) who talk about your industry.

Step four – If you have a reseller or distribution channel, develop a consistent communication strategy that helps educate and empower them to sell your products and services more effectively.

Step five – Take the persona developed in step two to build out a content strategy that's focuses on the prospects pain points and matches each piece of content to the buyer's journey (requires a content assessment):

- Learn – I think I have a problem.
- Solve – How do I solve that problem?
- Compare – Am I solving that problem the right way?
- Purchase – Help me make a purchase decision.
- Loyalty – Show me you appreciate me as a customer.

To create a Strategic Road Map, consider tools like:

- Cintell for persona development and distribution.
- Buzzsumo for content ideation.
- Followerwonk to help find social influencers.
- Social123 to find matching personas and profiles on LinkedIn.
- Right On Interactive's marketing automation platform to help manage the complete customer lifecycle from awareness to loyalty.

Sales Hack contributed by: Shawn Elledge, CEO Integrated Marketing Summit & CEO Sales Lead Automation

After years of hosting marketing events for the Kansas City Business

Marketing Association and being a quest speaker at various events around North America, I decided to launch an event series focused on Integrated Marketing Strategies. The Integrated Marketing Summit (IMS) is the premier event series dedicated to the continued education of advertising and marketing professionals.

Shawn's goal is to help companies drive revenue rapidly in this ever complicated world of instant and global communication.

BONUS SALES HACK #7
PROCESS SUCKS, KILL MANUAL

The real secret is even though process sucks, if you don't have one, your results will, too. The reason process sucks is that it is typically a load of monotonous manual tasks tied together by a workflow and tempo. Nobody does it consistently. It is only evaluated by how many deals you get (which is very far removed from the process—meaning there could have been other things that affected deals other than the process). Typically, the touch points become onerous once you get over a handful of accounts.

Everyone knows you need have activity volume that process dictates to be successful. Everyone also knows that personalization dramatically boosts effectiveness. What you need to hack is how to balance the time it takes to personalize with the time it takes to have high activity volume. Unfortunately, by strong arming people with process, companies create an either/or situation when it should be a both/and.

Here's how to have process AND personalization:

1   Define clear predictors and signs that point to GREAT prospects, using the demo-/firmographics of your current customers.
2   Segment each load of leads or lead you create by these predictors into Prime Contacts and Secondary Contacts.
3   Put Prime Contacts into a hybrid manual/automated workflow in Outreach so you can consistently do personalized manual tasks on key accounts.
4   Put Secondary Contacts into heavily automated workflows using tools like Outreach so you can capture low-hanging fruit and enable people who are interested to wave a flag for you to engage them.

This hack allows you to skyrocket activity that follows an automated process you build in Outreach while you are doing extremely personalized activity pushed to you by a manual/automated Outreach workflow.

Sales Hack contributed by: Mark Kosoglow, Vice President of Sales, Outreach.io

Mark is a commercially and technically astute transformational business & sales leader with over 18 years of experience in providing strategic

management oversight for fulfilling business goals while furthering business objectives to new heights. Mark is big-picture visionary in all facets of sales, business development, and account management with a track record of improving business performance, managing change, and turning around operations in a fiercely competitive business scenario.

BONUS SALES HACK #8
THE MARK BENIOFF HACK

Given that Tom Siebel has an ego the size of Jupiter, he was easy pickings for Marc Benioff's Salesforce.com. On page 39 of his book *Behind the Cloud*, Marc kindly gives me credit for creating his attack on Siebel with the now famous "I will not give my lunch money to Siebel" ad. According to one Siebel lieutenant, Tom went completely crazy and never recovered. And when he talked to reporters from various publications, he said that he would NOT advertise with anyone who would run such a scurrilous ad. You can see a hi-res copy of the ad on m website: http://www.rickbennett.com. Enjoy.

Of course, not all "sales hacks" work as planned. Just before Salesforce's 2012 Dreamforce conference, a company wanted to make a splash at the show. So I created an ad where "Marc Benioff for President" was spray painted on a brick wall. Yes, it got a lot of attention. Unfortunately, everyone kept asking Marc about his presidential campaign when he was trying to sell his CHAT feature. Marc wasn't pleased, and I never heard from the client again. You can also see that ad on the above website.

Sales Hack contributed by: Rick Bennett, Owner, Rick Bennett Advertising & PR

Rick specializes in guerrilla warfare marketing. Two of his most spectacular successes are Oracle and Salesforce.com. Rick's goal: find some  engineer/programmer in a garage who's been so nose-down on his task that he will be surprised when I exclaim, "Wow, you really don't know what you have, do you?" I think the fate of the world lies in superior new technology, not in politicians or the political process.

ABOUT THE "SALES HACKS"

Chad Burmeister, Vice President of Sales & Marketing, ConnectAndSell (Twitter handle: @SalesHack)

Chad has been voted as a Top 25 Most Influential Inside Sales Professional by the American Association of Inside Sales Professionals 6 years in a row – 2010, 2011, 2012, 2013, 2014, and 2015.

Chad is a regular speaker at conferences including SalesForce.com Dreamforce, The American Association of Inside Sales Professionals, and LeadsCon, and has had articles published in Fortune Magazine, Inc. Magazine, Selling Power Magazine, and more. Chad is an avid blogger at www.ConnectAndSell.com/salesvelocity and www.SalesHack.com.

Chris Beall, CEO, ConnectAndSell (Twitter handle: @chris8649)

Chris has been participating in software startups as a founder or at a very early stage for most of the past 30 years. Chris's focus has consistently been

on creating and taking to market simple products that can be used successfully the first time they are touched, without taking a course or reading a manual. Chris deeply believes that the most powerful part of any software system is the human being that we inappropriately call a "user", and that the value key in software is to let the computer do what it does well (go fast without getting bored) in order to free up human potential. The process of finding these solutions is more one of discovery than invention, and Chris has been lucky enough to have stumbled on a few of them.

In Memory of William "Bill" Ward Kingery
Born: December 14, 1945 - July 10, 2015

Family friend and CEO of Wireless Broadcasting Systems of America who offered Chad his first sales position

"Don't Fence Me In"

Oh, give me land, lots of land under starry skies above
Don't fence me in
Let me ride through the wide open country that I love
Don't fence me in

Let me be by myself in the evenin' breeze
And listen to the murmur of the cottonwood trees
Send me off forever but I ask you please
Don't fence me in

Just turn me loose, let me straddle my old saddle
Underneath the western skies
On my cayuse, let me wander over yonder
Till I see the mountains rise

I want to ride to the ridge where the West commences
And gaze at the moon till I lose my senses
And I can't look at hobbles and I can't stand fences
Don't fence me in

Oh, give me land, lots of land under starry skies
Don't fence me in
Let me ride through the wide country that I love
Don't fence me in

Let me be by myself in the evenin' breeze
And listen to the murmur of the cottonwood trees
Send me off forever but I ask you please
Don't fence me in

Just turn me loose, let me straddle my old saddle
Underneath the western skies
On my cayuse, let me wander over yonder
Till I see the mountains rise

I want to ride to the ridge where the West commences
And gaze at the moon till I lose my senses
And I can't look at hobbles and I can't stand fences

Don't fence me in, no
Pop, oh don't you fence me in.

Lyrics By Cole Porter